D1076636

PC Interfacing using USB

Other Titles of Interest

BP523	Easy PC Interfacing
BP531	Easy PC Upgrading
BP534	Build Your Own PC
BP541	Boost Your PC's Performance
BP542	Easy PC Case Modding
BP549	Easy PC Wi-Fi Networking
BP556	How to Transfer Computer Data and Settings

PC Interfacing using USB

Peter Bates

Bernard Babani (publishing) Ltd
The Grampians
Shepherds Bush Road
London W6 7NF
England
www.babanibooks.com

Please note

Important note

Due to processes used in preparing and printing this book, the accuracy of the PCB track layout dimensions cannot be guaranteed. A graticule is provided by the drawings to help in this matter.

First Published – May 2003

Reprinted – March 2005

British Library Cataloguing in Publication Data

A catalogue record for this book is available from the British Library

ISBN 0 85934 535 1

Cover Design by Gregor Arthur

Printed and bound in Great Britain by Cox & Wyman Ltd

Preface

Interfacing to PCs has been around for many years but to many people it is still a mystery as to how data can be transmitted to and from a PC and the outside world. This book has been designed for both the beginner and the expert to interfacing. The only prerequisite is a reasonable knowledge of Visual Basic, though to some extent an ability to write very simple Visual Basic programs may be adequate if the user is proficient in the knowledge of other computer programs.

The book is built around an interfacing module that is connected to the USB port of a PC. This means that there is no delving around inside the PC which has prevented many beginners even embarking on interfacing in the past. Some background to the USB standard is presented and also details are introduced as to how the USB interface module is programmed.

In the past the normal method of interfacing was to use the Intel 8255A Programmable Peripheral Interface and to many of those experienced in interfacing this has become the standard approach to the task. Interface cards being produced at the current time use the same mode of programming so that it seemed natural to transfer those programming techniques over to the USB interface module. This will enable experts to quickly grasp how to program the USB interface module and provide the beginner with all the rudiments of interfacing to be able to go off and do their projects as quickly as possible.

Once the fundamentals of getting data in and out of the USB interface module have been dealt with, the book then looks at five different areas of use for it. Each of these areas has an interface board to accompany it and full constructional details are provided including details of the pcb, the components required and any necessary calibration details.

Ideally the reader should move through the book sequentially performing all the programs but once chapters 1 to 3 have been read, it is possible to dip into any of the remaining chapters in any order. The purpose of the book is to stimulate an interest in interfacing and studying the programs will help most users to understand the principles that are being presented.

Once all the fundamentals have been learnt both beginners and experts will be able to use stepper motors, DACs and ADCs in a variety of projects. The important point always to observe is to save your program before running it. This will prevent a vast amount of frustration and you will always be in a position to correct the odd typo which so often creeps into a program.

I should like to take this opportunity to thank my former colleagues Eric Webster and Maurice Rhodes, both recently retired, for their contributions to all our knowledge about interfacing. Also to the technical support of Alan Kent, Helen Poulton, Barbara Ridding and Rick Collins from the Department of Physics, Astronomy and Mathematics of the University of Central Lancashire for their assistance in maintaining the PCs, making pcbs, soldering components and testing circuit boards and generally being very nice to everyone when things have not been going well.

In addition I must acknowledge Margaret and Victoria who have both been extremely tolerant of my enthusiasm for PC interfacing which has developed over many years and has gone through many highs and lows. I believe that this book illustrates one of the highs.

Peter Bates

About the Author

Peter Bates is currently the Course Leader of the MSc in PC Interfacing in the Department of Physics, Astronomy and Mathematics at the University of Central Lancashire, Preston, UK. He is a physics graduate who went on to obtain a PhD in solid-state physics from Bangor University and in over 30 years he has taught physics, solid-state physics and microcomputer interfacing at all levels from A-level through to postgraduate. His interest in electronics developed as a consequence of being asked to teach the subject in 1974 when he was appointed to the Department of Physics at Preston Polytechnic.

Peter's expertise in interfacing sensors, transducers and instruments to computers was the foundation of the MSc in PC Interfacing in which he is responsible for teaching fundamental interfacing and virtual instrumentation using Microsoft Visual Basic and National Instruments LabVIEW.

His hobbies are quite diverse ranging from hi-fi and music to DIY and gardening.

Trademarks

Contents

3

Programming the Module 25

4

Digital Input/Output 41

1

What is USB?

The Universal Serial Bus

The Universal Serial Bus (USB) is an interfacing bus that is now becoming standard on all types of PC. It was introduced by Microsoft in Windows 98 and has subsequently been supported in Windows 2000, XP and ME but not in Windows NT. Its popularity has increased because of the relative ease with which it can be used and the range of hardware devices which incorporate it. These include printers, scanners, digital cameras, mice, keyboards, joysticks, etc. It is extremely popular with laptops because of the small size of its sockets and it is becoming common on desktop PCs as well. It is not beyond the realms of possibility that USB could easily replace the RS232 interface as the preferred serial interface.

USB features

USB is a serial data transmission system in which the data stream is time-shared. This means that all the devices, i.e. mice, keyboard, printers, etc., connected to the PC are polled regularly at 1ms intervals by the PC and in its 1ms time interval the device can place data on to the bus. Each device has a unique address allocated by the PC and up to 127 devices can be connected to the USB at any one time.

The speed of data transmission is dependent upon the version of USB being used. The latest version USB2.0 has a speed of 460Mbits/s whilst the older version USB1.1 supports two speeds 12Mbit/s and 1.5Mbits/s. In the latter case the two speeds can co-exist together on the same wire and the speed is determined in the hardware of the device. USB2.0 interfaces fitted to PCs can support devices using USB1.1 but it is questionable whether USB2.0 devices can be used with USB1.1 PC interfaces.

USB connectors and cables

The USB interface inside a PC is made up of a USB controller which is a set of chips that provide the interface between the hardware and the applications software resident in the PC. Within the PC is a host hub to which all the devices connected to the USB system connect. A PC normally has at least two connectors mounted on its case which connect to this host hub and users can then purchase further hubs which can provide additional ports for up to 127 devices.

The cables, made up of 4 conductors, are used to connect devices to these hubs. Two types of USB connectors are used; Type A and Type B and these are illustrated in Figure 1.1.

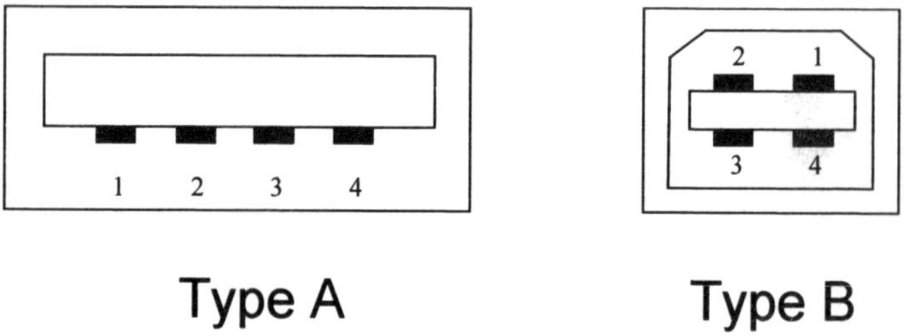

Figure 1.1 USB connectors

Normally a Type A socket is fitted to a PC and a device has a Type B. The connectors are different to indicate the normal flow of communication which may either be *upstream* or *downstream*.

Two of the four conductors in the cable are differential data lines and the other two are 5V and GND. Figure 1.2 shows the configuration of the cable.

A feature of the USB plugs is that pins 1 and 4, the supply lines, are slightly longer than the data lines. This means that when the plug is inserted into the socket, the supply is connected before the data. This not only reduces the risk of damage due to electrostatic charge but provides the USB feature of being able to connect and disconnect devices without having to power down the PC. The purpose of the supply lines is to provide power for the USB devices which are connected to the bus but in the main this is limited to them drawing no more than 450mA. In most cases the device, e.g. printer, will need to be provided with its own power supply.

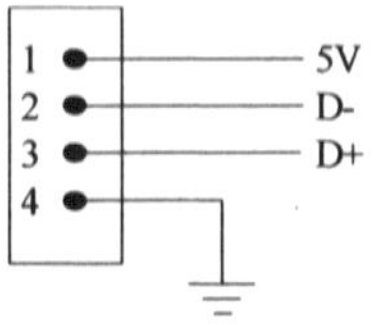

Figure 1.2 USB cable configuration

The two data lines, D+ and D–, are used to send either data or commands. A 1 bit is sent when D+ is high and D– is low and a 0 bit when D– is high and D+ is low.

USB data communication

USB devices contain a CPU, i.e. a microprocessor, a microcontroller, etc., which is used to control the communication process. Each device has a number of buffers which are used to store data prior to transmission to the PC or to store data received from the PC. These are referred to as IN and OUT endpoints and a device can have up to a maximum of 16 of each.

The device's CPU pre- and post-processing ability provides the flexibility and standardisation of the USB system. Essentially it is an extension of the PC's BIOS and it is possible to plug a USB mouse or keyboard into a PC and for it to start immediately using the generic data held within the PC. There is no need to load specialised drivers which cause so many problems in installing software on a PC. It must be stated that with specialised devices, drivers are necessary and these are provided in an .INF file which is normally loaded in response to the Plug 'n Play Wizard.

The IN endpoint of a device is the buffer into which data obtained from the device itself is placed and the OUT endpoint is the buffer in which data from the PC is placed so that it can be accessed by the device.

Figure 1.3 (based upon a diagram by *J Hyde (1999)*) is a schematic of how the endpoints interface to the PC via the device drivers.

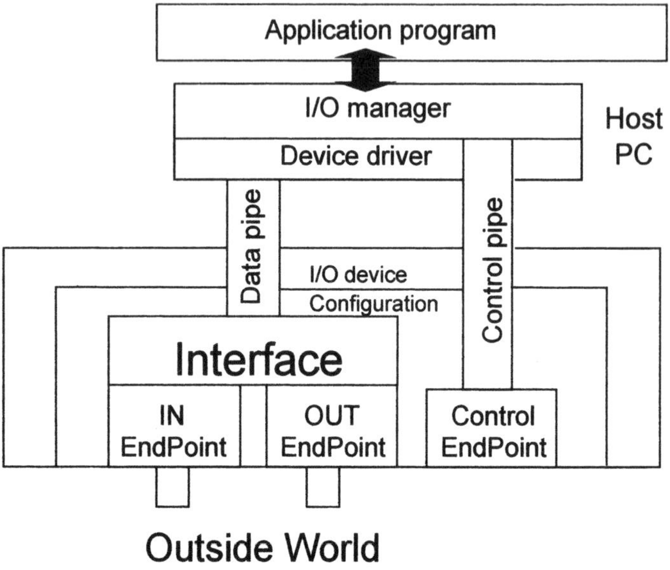

Figure 1.3 USB interface model

The device also has the control endpoint which is bi-directional and is used to identify the device, discover its capabilities and also control it. When the USB device is attached, a conversation takes place on the control endpoint so that the device can be integrated into the operating environment of the PC. This *enumeration* involves pre-formatted standard USB requests and these have to be provided in software design.

It will be seen from Figure 1.3 that communication between the device and the PC takes place using pipes. These pipes are implemented in the USB cable by using different types of packets of data. It is the application program which opens devices and the operating system that implements the low-level communication to the device. From the device point of view, data arrives from the PC into the OUT endpoint and the supplied data from the device is put into the IN endpoint.

Putting it all together

When a USB device is plugged into a port there is a voltage change on one of the two data lines. If D+ goes high the device is a high speed device, i.e. printer, scanner, etc., and the data that is transmitted within the 1ms packets is sent at 12Mbit/s. If D– goes high the device is a low-speed device, i.e. keyboard, mouse, etc., and the data is transmitted at 1.5Mbit/s.

A polling signal is then sent to the device requesting it to identify itself. The device responds with its own product and vendor Ids, i.e. the PID and VID. Windows then searches its directories for the correct driver for the device and if one cannot be found it requests one to be loaded. Once the driver is loaded the application programme then proceeds. The ability to connect and disconnect a USB device without switching off the PC is a distinct advantage when developing interfacing software as it often enables the interface to clear any corrupted settings very quickly and easily.

The device is now part of the USB system with the PC being the master and the device being a slave.The PC polls devices to issue commands, request whether the device is ready to send or receive data and to be apportioned a time slice so that the device can transmit data upstream to the PC at regular time intervals.

The PC's messages consist of three packets: a token packet, a data packet and a handshaking packet. The token packet contains an address and since the message is sent to all devices on the bus it is only the device whose address matches the token's address that will respond to it. The device then can send its data when the PC gives its permission.

Types of data

There are three types of data transfer between the PC and USB device and these are assigned priorities according to certain criteria.

Isochronous

This is real-time data transfer and has the highest priority. It is the transfer of a large amount of data where there can be no interruptions and there is no error checking provided. It is used for video and sound data which require large data transfers and can absorb some data loss.

Interrupt

This is used for keyboards, mice and joysticks which are low-speed data devices.They generate occasional interrupts and then transmit small amounts of data quickly. The priority is not as high as isochronous.

Bulk

This is used for the transfer of a large amount of data when speed is not of importance. It has low priority and is used for printers, scanners and digital cameras.

There is a fourth data transfer mode which is called Control transfer. All USB devices support it and it has high priority and has error checking built in. It is used to provide initialisation information but there are occasions when it can be used for low-speed data transfer.

Summary

USB is a data transfer standard which enables a range of different devices to be attached to and removed from a PC without switching it off. Data is transferred to the PC in 1ms frames at speeds of 1.5Mbit/s, 12Mbit/s and even 460Mbit/s in the latest USB2.0 version. A well-defined set of protocols are used for data transfer and with the aid of external hubs it is possible to connect up to 127 devices to a USB port.

The prospects of using USB to interface suitable devices capable of being used in instrumentation could be beneficial, as it would enable devices to be portable between PCs without having to provide plug-in cards. In addition it could also be extremely cost effective as most PCs are supplied with USB ports built in.

References

J Hyde, *USB Design by Example*, (1999) J Wiley, New York

T Wong, '*Understanding USB*' (November 1999), *Electronics World*

E Insam, '*USB made easy*' (February 2002), *Electronics World*

http://www.usb.org - web site of the USB organisation

2

USB I/O 24 Module

USB devices

USB devices have become very popular with PC users as they can be easily connected and disconnected from the PC whilst it is still switched on. Consequently printers, scanners, cameras and even measuring instruments are being provided with USB interfaces. The major handicap to those of us who wish to develop instrumentation or simply to experiment with USB has been the complexity and cost of the electronics required to enable USB signals to be either generated or captured.

This problem has now been surmounted with the appearance of several ICs with the capabilities of coping with the USB protocols in a similar manner to the UARTs that are used with RS232. UARTs (Universal Asynchronous Receiver Transmitter devices) can convert the serial RS232 signal into 8-bit parallel and vice versa and also deal with the handshaking requirements of the RS232 standard. A typical example of such a USB integrated circuit is the FT8U245 manufactured by Future Technology Devices International (FTDI) of Glasgow, Scotland.

The FT8U245

The FT8U245 is capable of sending and receiving USB data at up to 1MByte/s. The 8-bit parallel output/input port is connected to a 384-byte FIFO transmit buffer/128-byte FIFO receive buffer (Figure 2.1).

All the USB protocols are handled within the integrated circuit so that the user does not have to become involved in any complex programming to pass data to and from the device. In fact FTDI provide a USB driver for the system which ensures that the user can interact with the device with relative ease. The 8-bit I/O port of the FT8U245 is designed to be interfaced to any microcontroller using either the memory I/O map of the microcontroller using DMA, or by controlling the I/O ports.

The device has many commercial applications ranging from USB ISDN and ADSL modems to high-speed USB instrumentation.

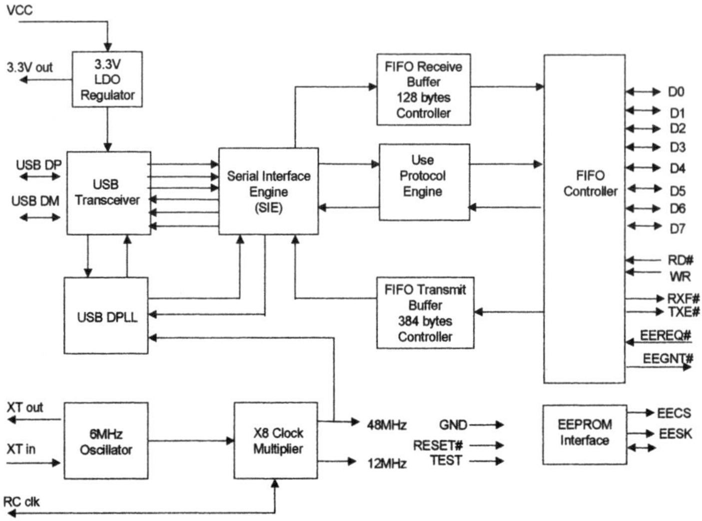

Figure 2.1 FT8U245 Block Diagram (Simplified)

The USB I/O 24 module

The 8-bit I/O of the FT8U245 has limitations as far as the experimenter is concerned because there are many sensors and transducers which require control line facilities over and above the 8 data lines and these are not easy to implement with handshaking lines that are more suited for use with a microcontroller. The obvious answer is to use a microcontroller, but once again that can cause problems with experimenters who may not wish to learn to program microcontrollers or who have not got access to the equipment necessary to perform such tasks. Fortunately Ravar Pty Ltd of Queensland, Australia produce a USB 24-line general-purpose Input Output module based upon the FTDI FT8U245 IC.

The USB I/O 24 module (Figure 2.2) has 24 independently programmable I/O pins in three groups of 8.

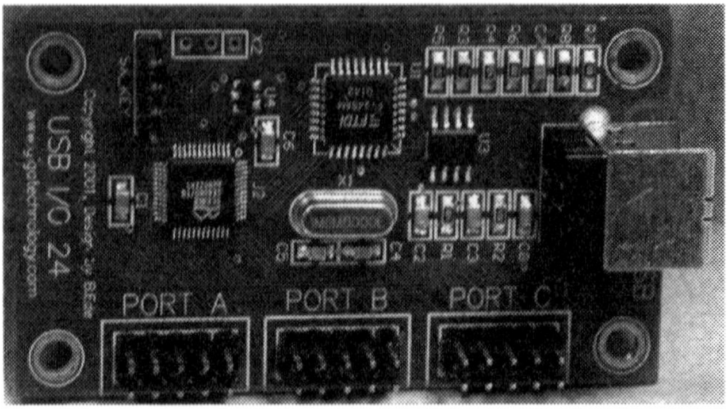

Figure 2.2 The USB I/O 24 module

The module is based on the FTDI FT8U245 USB IC and a UNICOM SAC48 microcontroller and is capable of transfer rates up to 250,000 8-bit port reads or writes per second. A Virtual COM Port Driver is available for a range of operating systems, so that the device can be accessed as a normal serial port which can be programmed in any of the popular programming languages. This means that when the module is connected to the USB port of the PC it is automatically recognised and will accordingly appear in the COM section of the Device Manager of Windows when Windows 98, 2000, ME or XP is used.

The module is USB1.1 Specification compliant and the USB VID, PID, Serial Number and Product is recognised and displayed. The on-board EEPROM and FLASH Microcontroller can be re-programmed according to whatever the user may require but in most cases the provided firmware data is more than satisfactory.

Each I/O pin can be configured individually as an input or output. An input pin is TTL level compatible and an output pin can sink or source up to 30mA. The device is connected to the USB port of the PC using a suitable cable. This normally has a Type A USB connector to the PC and a Type B to the module. The module is powered from the USB with up to 450mA available current. This means that the USB I/O 24 Module can be used in a range of user applications without the need of an external power supply to drive peripherals.

The USB I/O 24 module Connectors

The USB I/O 24 module has its 24 I/O pins distributed into three eight-pin ports A, B and C. Each port has two additional pins which are used for +5V and a ground. The description for the ten pins in each port is shown in Table 2.1.

Pin	Signal	Description
1	+5V	USB bus supply
2	I/O8	Programmable I/O pin with bit value of 128
3	I/O7	Programmable I/O pin with bit value of 64
4	I/O6	Programmable I/O pin with bit value of 32
5	I/O5	Programmable I/O pin with bit value of 16
6	I/O4	Programmable I/O pin with bit value of 8
7	I/O3	Programmable I/O pin with bit value of 4
8	I/O2	Programmable I/O pin with bit value of 2
9	I/O1	Programmable I/O pin with bit value of 1
10	GND	USB bus and I/O ground

Table 2.1 Description of USB I/O 24 Port Connector

The pins are distributed in each port according to Figure 2.3. and Figure 2.4 shows the three ports arranged on the USB 24 I/O module.

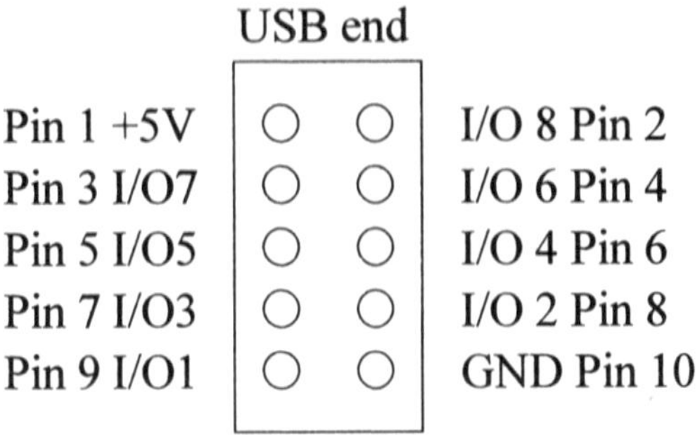

Figure 2.3 USB I/O 24 Port Connector pin configuration

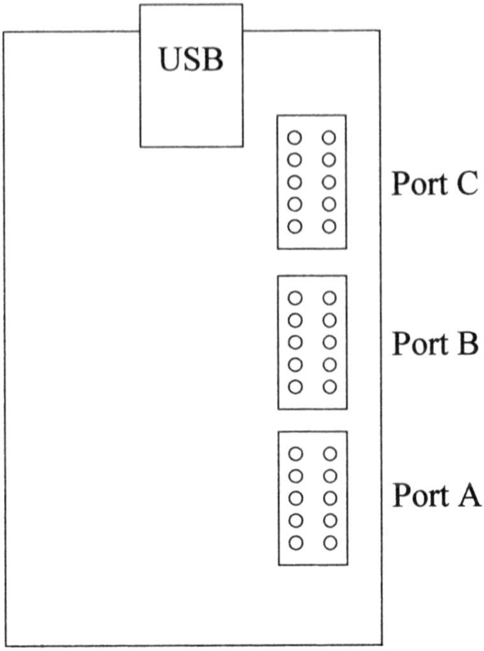

Figure 2.4 USB I/O 24 port layout

The USB I/O 24 module Command Protocol

The USB I/O 24 module has a set of commands which enable the individual ports to be configured as either inputs or outputs. In addition data can be read from or written to each of the ports. There is also a command that can be used to identify the device which is connected to the USB port. These commands are summarised in Table 2.2.

Command	Data	Function
?	Transmits 'ISB I/O 24'	Identify Device
!A	1 byte port I/O data	Write to Port A direction register
!B	1 byte port I/O data	Write to Port B direction register
!C	1 byte port I/O data	Write to Port C direction register
A	Port A data	Write to Port A
B	Port B data	Write to Port B
C	Port C data	Write to Port C
a	Port A data	Read to Port A
b	Port B data	Read to Port B
c	Port C data	Read to Port C

Table 2.2 USB I/O 24 commands

Before the ports can be used they must be initially configured either as an output or as an input.

The syntax to set port A as an output is :

```
PortI/Ostring = "!A"+Chr$(0)
```

Port A is set as an input with the following statement:

```
PortI/Ostring = "!A"+Chr$(255)
```

In both of these examples all Port A pins are set in the same direction. In many applications it is possible to have a mix of pins being both inputs and outputs:

PortI/OString = "!A"+Chr$(&02)

This sets pin 2 as an output and all other pins as inputs.

The task of reading Port A is achieved using:

DataString = "a"

and to write data to Port A the following statement is used:

DataString = "A"+Chr$(128).

In the former case, data is placed into the variable Datastring. In the latter case Pin 8 is set high and all other pins are low.

The examples given above can also be performed for ports B and C.

Using USB I/O 24 Command Protocols

The USB I/O 24 module is very versatile with its 24 I/O pins and to some extent that is its major downfall especially for beginners to interfacing. There is almost an infinite number of ways in which the module can be used and it is difficult to decide how to begin and to ensure success. To the experienced user who can draw upon the techniques and programs used with other types of interface cards and modules used with the PC there are certain rules which have aided them in the past. In general these are:

1. Configure the interface card for input or output
2. Read from or write to the interface

Close examination of devices attached to other commercial interface cards reveal that in many cases 8 data lines and 2 control lines will suffice to create reliable operation. With 24 I/O lines it would appear that two such devices could be supported.

In fact 24 I/O lines divided into 3 ports is almost an industry standard and can be traced back to the Intel 8255A Programmable Peripheral

Interface (PPI). The PPI was used as the parallel I/O device with Intel microprocessors used in the original IBM PCs.

The feature of the 8255A was that it could be programmed to operate in three distinct modes. Two of the modes, 1 and 2, involved complex handshaking processes but Mode 0 was very similar to the USB I/O 24 module with 24 lines which could be configured as inputs or outputs divided into three ports A, B and C. The method of programming the 8255A in Mode 0 will aid us in programming the USB I/O 24 module.

How Mode 0 of the 8255A is programmed

Mode 0 of the 8255A takes the 24 I/O lines and divides them into two groups A and B. Group A consists of all the lines of Port A plus the four upper lines of Port C (i.e. I/O8, I/O7, I/O6 and I/O5 of Port C). Group B consists of all the lines of Port B plus the four lower lines of Port C (i.e. I/O4, I/O3, I/O2 and I/O1 of Port C). Figure 2.5 illustrates this distribution of I/O lines.

Group A		Group B	
Port A	Port C (Upper)	Port B	Port C (Lower)
I/O 1 - 8	I/O 5 - 8	I/O 1-8	I/O 1 - 4

Figure 2.5 Distribution of 8255A I/O lines for Mode 0 operation

In many applications Ports A and B will be used for data and the upper and lower groupings of Port C can be used for control lines. Programming is then further simplified by each of the sub-groups shown in Figure 2.5 being configured as inputs or outputs. This alleviates the problem of programming each I/O line individually and Chapter 3 will show the advantages of programming the groups of I/O lines.

Programming the 8255A involved configuring the device with an 8-bit control word. Each bit of the control word has a significance which is shown in Figure 2.6.

Control word

D7	D6	D5	D4	D3	D2	D1	D0
Mode set flag	Mode selection		Port A	Port C (Upper)	Mode selection	Port A	Port C (Lower)
1=Active	00=Mode0 01=Mode1 1X=Mode2		1=i/p 0=o/p	1=i/p 0=o/p	0=Mode0 1=Mode1	1=i/p 0=o/p	1=i/p 0=o/p
	Group A				Group B		

Figure 2.6 8255A mode definition format

Inserting the Mode 0 settings simplifies the control word (Figure 2.7)

Control word

1	0	0	D4	D3	0	D1	D0
			Port A	Port C (Upper)		Port B	Port C (Lower)
			1=i/p 0=o/p	1=i/p 0=o/p		1=i/p 0=o/p	1=i/p 0=o/p

Figure 2.7 8255A mode 0 control word

Port A, Port B and the two parts of Port C can now be set as inputs or outputs simply by setting the bits D_4, D_3, D_1 and D_0. These settings are then added to the setting bit D_7 which is already set to 1. This means adding decimal 128 to those other bits in the control word which are required to set the Port direction.

The net result is shown in Table 2.3 which indicates the control word codes required to configure the 8255A for Mode 0 operation.

Port A	Port C (Upper)	Port B	Port C (Lower)	Code (decimal)
Output	Output	Output	Output	128
Output	Output	Output	Input	129
Output	Output	Input	Output	130
Output	Output	Input	Input	131
Output	Input	Output	Output	136
Output	Input	Output	Input	137
Output	Input	Input	Output	138
Output	Input	Input	Input	139
Input	Output	Output	Output	144
Input	Output	Output	Input	145
Input	Output	Input	Output	146
Input	Output	Input	Input	147
Input	Input	Output	Output	152
Input	Input	Output	Input	153
Input	Input	Input	Output	154
Input	Input	Input	Input	155

Table 2.3 8255A control word Mode 0 settings

Why use the 8255A settings?

The peculiar code settings are initially strange to the beginner but reference to Table 2.3 becomes second nature and ensures reliable programming of the chip in the future. In addition commercial 24-line digital I/O boards used with the ISA and PCI slots in PCs are often based upon the 8255A or its derivatives so that any programs written for one system should be portable to any of the other systems. Also if a suitable library program is written, either in C or Visual Basic, the task of programming the interface board becomes fairly easy. This is the task that will be tackled in Chapter 3 when the code settings are applied to the USB I/O 24 module.

The 8255A registers

There are four registers in the 8255A which are used to hold Port A, Port B, Port C and the Control Register data. Each of these registers can be addressed provided the base address of the 8255A device is known. Usually the 8255A sits on a card which is plugged into the I/O slot of the PC and the registers are allocated addresses from the PC's memory. In the case of the USB I/O 24 module mimicking the 8255A, the base address of the registers can be taken as 0. This means that the registers and the Ports, etc., have the following address allocations and functions.

Address	Register	Function	Lines
0	Port A	i/p / o/p data	PA0 – PA7
1	Port B	i/p / o/p data	PB0 – PB7
2	Port C	Control lines	CA1,CA2,CB1,CB2
3	Control	Control register	

Table 2.4 Port and register addresses

The Control Lines

Port C has been divided into upper and lower sub-groups which can be programmed as inputs or outputs. Examination of applications of 8255A interface boards reveal that one line from the upper group and one line from the lower group are assigned to Port A and a similar arrangement is found for Port B. Table 2.5 shows a typical arrangement.

High							Low
7	6	5	4	3	2	1	0
		CB2	CA2			CB1	CA1

Table 2.5 Arrangement of Port C

It can be seen that the upper sub-group contributes bit 4 as control line CA2 and the lower sub-group contributes bit 0 as CA1 to Port A. Similarly Port B gets bits 5 and 1 as CB2 and CB1 respectively. Table 2.6 shows both the binary and hexadecimal code required to have all possible combinations of these four control lines providing output signals.

Binary Pattern	Hex	Decimal	CB2	CA2	CB1	CA1
0000 0000	00	0	OFF	OFF	OFF	OFF
0000 0001	01	1	OFF	OFF	OFF	ON
0000 0010	02	2	OFF	OFF	ON	OFF
0000 0011	03	3	OFF	OFF	ON	ON
0001 0000	10	16	OFF	ON	OFF	OFF
0001 0001	11	17	OFF	ON	OFF	ON
0001 0010	12	18	OFF	ON	ON	OFF
0001 0011	13	19	OFF	ON	ON	ON
0010 0000	20	32	ON	OFF	OFF	OFF
0010 0001	21	33	ON	OFF	OFF	ON
0010 0010	22	34	ON	OFF	ON	OFF
0010 0011	23	35	ON	OFF	ON	ON
0011 0000	30	48	ON	ON	OFF	OFF
0011 0001	31	49	ON	ON	OFF	ON
0011 0010	32	50	ON	ON	ON	OFF
0011 0011	33	51	ON	ON	ON	ON

Table 2.6 Control line settings (Outputs)

Connections to the USB I/O 24 module

The net result of considering all these aspects of using the 8255A PPI is that the 24 lines of the USB I/O 24 module can be divided into 8 data lines of Port A with 2 control lines CA1 and CA2 and 8 data lines of Port B with 2 control lines CB1 and CB2. Associated with these pairings will be a +5V supply line and a GND line making 12 lines associated with Port A and 12 lines associated with Port B. These lines are to be connected to the different interface boards used in the following chapters and Figure 2.8 shows the wiring harness that is required for the purpose with the connections shown in Tables 2.7 and 2.8.

The 20-way IDC sockets (RS 192-7388) provide the Ports A and B connections and the 10-way header sockets (RS 360-6220) are used to connect the USB I/O 24 module. (All sockets are viewed from the rear.)

20-way IDC		10-way header	
Pin	**Function**	**Header**	**Pin**
2	CA1	C1	9
4	CA2	C5	5
6	PA0	A1	9
8	PA1	A2	8
10	PA2	A3	7
12	PA3	A4	6
14	PA4	A5	5
16	PA5	A6	4
18	PA6	A7	3
20	PA7	A8	2
1	+5V	+5V	1
19	0V	0V	10

Table 2.7 Port A connections

20-way IDC		10-way header	
Pin	**Function**	**Header**	**Pin**
2	CB1	C2	8
4	CB2	C6	4
6	PB0	B1	9
8	PB1	B2	8
10	PB2	B3	7
12	PB3	B4	6
14	PB4	B5	5
16	PB5	B6	4
18	PB6	B7	3
20	PB7	B8	2
1	+5V	+5V	1
19	0V	0V	10

Table 2.8 Port B connections

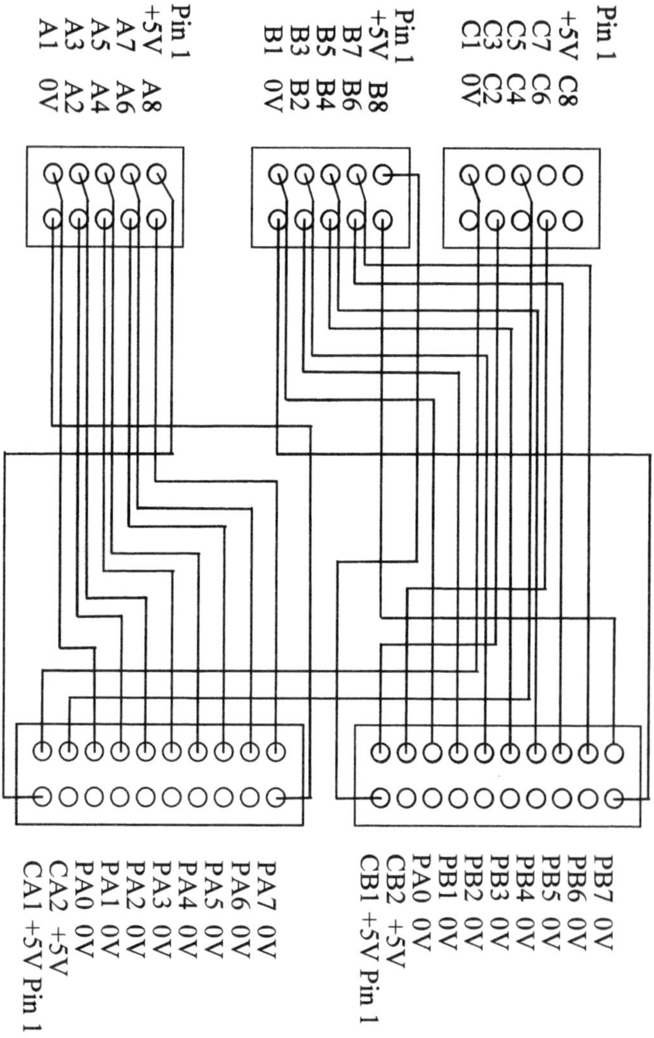

Figure 2.8 Method of wiring the USB I/O 24 module for use with the interface boards

Summary

The USB I/O 24 module is designed to enable digital input/output signals to be interfaced to the USB port of a PC. The interface cards that can be used with ISA and PCI slots of PCs are based upon the Intel 8255A PPI and it is possible to configure the USB I/O 24 module to mimic this device. This means that programs already written for the 8255A will be compatible with the USB I/O 24 module and, provided a suitable cable harness is used, it is possible for interface boards developed for the 8255A to be used with the USB I/O 24 module.

The next stage of the process is to write a universal Visual Basic module that can store the library of calls that will achieve these tasks.

3

Programming the Module

The case for the USB I/O 24 Module

The USB I/O 24 module can be programmed either with serial device commands or by using a DLL which enables function calls to be made to it. Basically the mode of interface interaction is the same but with the serial method it is the user who has to ensure that all the correct protocol steps are made whilst with the DLL method the steps are contained within the DLL. In addition the serial communication rate is 115,200 Baud which means that the possibility of a communication breakdown occurring is very real so that for most applications the serial method is far from ideal. Using the DLL approach ensures a more reliable communication path.

The FT8U245 drivers

The USB I/O 24 module is driven by the FT8U245 IC and it is necessary to install its drivers on the PC. These drivers are obtainable from the FTDI website (http://www.ftdichip.com/support.htm). The drivers should be downloaded to a folder on the PC and then unzipped. When the USB I/O 24 module is plugged into the USB port the PC checks for suitable drivers and if none exist it will prompt the user to load the drivers. It is then a question of following the instructions that appear on the screen.

The instructions for installing drivers under Windows 98 differ from those for Windows 2000 and XP. Full Application Notes for the installation process can be downloaded from the FTDI web site. The two files that are loaded are a Windows Device Manager driver, FTD2XX.SYS and an Applications Software Interface, FTD2XX.DLL. Figure 3.1 indicates the driver architecture.

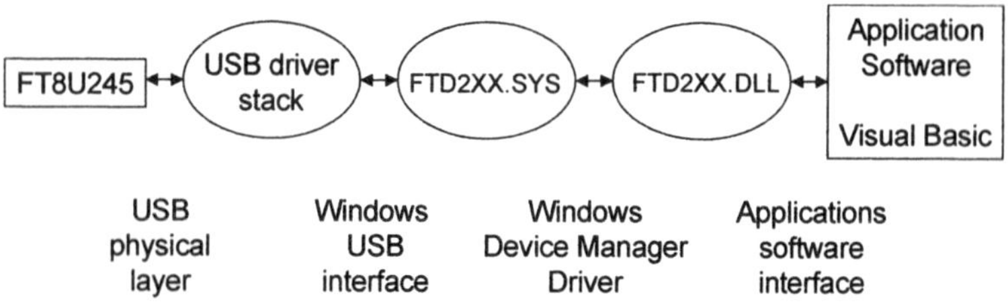

Figure 3.1 The FTDI D2XX Driver Architecture

These drivers can be used in conjunction with a range of different programming applications including Visual Basic, Visual C++, Delphi, etc. In addition to the FT8U245 IC the drivers can be used with the FT8U232 IC which is designed to convert USB signals to serial and vice versa. A comprehensive programmer's guide (FTD2XX Direct Driver Programmer's Guide, 27th July 2001) is available from the FTDI web site. This will assist experienced programmers to produce extremely complex programs using the USB I/O 24 module.

How to set up the FTDI D2XX Drivers

The two drivers that have been installed on your PC are not normally loaded unless the USB I/O 24 module is connected to the USB port. When the module is connected the arrow cursor will change to the egg-timer whilst the drivers are loaded and then revert back to the arrow after a short time. When the module is disconnected a similar process will take place.

Once the module is connected and the drivers are loaded, the FTDI FT8U2XX device is recognised in the USB controllers of the Device Manager of the PC. (Figure 3.2)

The Device Manager is accessed from **Control Panel / System**. It is possible to access the properties of the device by right-clicking on the mouse and checking that the driver is loaded and operational.

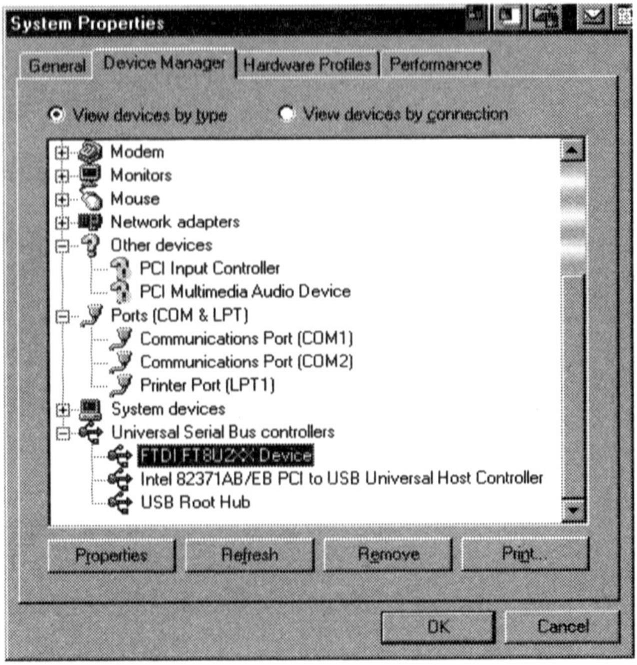

Figure 3.2 Device Manager Properties

The role of the DLL

A DLL is a Dynamic Linked Library. It is a file that contains functions or routines which a program can call upon whenever they are needed. Many applications programs, i.e. C, Basic, etc., use mathematical functions such as sin, cos, etc., which are built into the software. In the case of Visual Basic the mathematical function arcsin is not a recognised function and it is necessary for the user to write a little routine to calculate arcsin. Often the function is written in Visual Basic but it not unusual to write it in a language, e.g. C, which accepts mathematical manipulation more easily. This C program can then be compiled as a DLL which can be then called by the Visual Basic program. The feature of the DLL is that it is not loaded until it is required thus saving a great deal of memory space.

A driver DLL contains functions which enable a program to access a particular device which in the case of the FTD2XX.DLL is the USB I/O 24 module connected to the USB port. A feature of a function is that there are a number of parameters which are required within the function itself. It is important that the parameters are in the correct format otherwise an error will occur which could cause the PC to crash. This is one reason to ensure that whenever DLLs are being developed the program is saved before running or otherwise valuable work can be easily lost.

In order to ensure that the parameters passed to and from the DLL are correctly formatted, they have to be declared and this has to be done in a formal way. The Visual Basic code below illustrates this quite clearly:

```
Public Declare Function FT_Open Lib "FTD2XX.DLL" (ByVal
intDeviceNumber As Integer, ByRef lngHandle As Long) As Long
```

Public indicates that the function will be accessible from all parts of the Visual Basic project and the Function is FT_Open which is stored within the FTD2XX.DLL file. The two parameters that are being passed are quite different in their nature. The Device Number (intDeviceNumber) is an integer between –32768 and +32767 whose value is being passed to the function. The lngHandle is the port that is being opened for the device and ByRef indicates that it is the address of where that handle exists which is being passed to the function. Long indicates that the address lies between –214748348 and +2147483647. The As Long following the brackets indicates the number which is returned when the function is completed. Often either 1 or 0 is returned to indicate whether the function has completed its task successfully or not, though there are cases when a more meaningful number is returned.

Visual Basic code

It is assumed that the reader has some knowledge of Visual Basic and will not be too daunted by the next few sections.

A Visual Basic project consists of Forms and Modules. Forms are the visual parts that appear whenever the project runs and the module is similar to a BASIC program even to the extent of having a .bas extension. In the following chapters on interfacing you will find that the Forms are tailored to the devices that are being considered while a module, io_usb.bas will keep on appearing throughout the project. io_usb.bas is a module which contains all of the information which is required to communicate with the USB I/O 24 module.

In essence io_usb.bas contains the following parts:

1. Declarations
2. A read device routine (Readprog)
3. A write device routine (Writeprog)
4. Data transfer out (PortOut)
5. Data transfer in (PortIn)

Parts 1, 2 and 3 are Visual Basic code supplied by FTDI with some modifications, and would appear in any Visual Basic software developed for the FTDI FT8U245 IC. Parts 4 and 5 have been developed specifically for the USB I/O 24 module to mimic the 8255A PPI discussed in the previous chapter.

The next task is to type in the relevant code into the module io_usb.bas. This must be done carefully to avoid any errors otherwise it will be necessary to spend time debugging the code. All of this code is required and it cannot be tested until a suitable Form is produced. Type in each of the sections and ensure that you save at the end of each section. To make the task easier, each section will be introduced by a short explanation of what the code is doing.

Declarations

The first part of the Declarations involves declaring the four functions that are going to be used from the FTD2XXX.DLL. There are several other functions contained in this file which we will not need to use.

The first two declarations are concerned with opening and closing the port. The parameters being passed have already been explained.

The FT_Read and FT_Write functions are very similar with the appropriate port handle being selected, buffers for use of the variable being required and the size of the buffers being declared. The only difference is the addresses from where data is to be read and to where data is to be written.

```
'Declare FTD2XX functions

Public Declare Function FT_Open Lib "FTD2XX.DLL" (ByVal intDeviceNumber As Integer, ByRef lngHandle As Long) As Long

Public Declare Function FT_Close Lib "FTD2XX.DLL" (ByVal lngHandle As Long) As Long

Public Declare Function FT_Read Lib "FTD2XX.DLL" (ByVal lngHandle As Long, ByVal lpszBuffer As String, ByVal lngBufferSize As Long, ByRef lngBytesReturned As Long) As Long

Public Declare Function FT_Write Lib "FTD2XX.DLL" (ByVal lngHandle As Long, ByVal lpszBuffer As String, ByVal lngBufferSize As Long, ByRef lngBytesWritten As Long) As Long
```

There are a number of constants that are required in FTD2XX.DLL which have specific values and these are declared in the next section.

```
' Return codes
Const FT_OK = 0
Const FT_INVALID_HANDLE = 1
Const FT_DEVICE_NOT_FOUND = 2
Const FT_DEVICE_NOT_OPENED = 3
Const FT_IO_ERROR = 4
Const FT_INSUFFICIENT_RESOURCES = 5
```

The final part of the Declarations involves declaring a variable a$ which is to be used throughout the project, so that it is made Public and will reside in the io_usb.bas module.

```
' Declare variable
Public a$
```

Readprog

This is rather an involved section as it necessitates writing to the port with certain information and then reading the response. Surrounding these two processes the USB port is opened and closed.

Initially the parameters required by the four functions in the DLL are declared.

```
'Read port routine
Public Sub Readprog()
Dim lngHandle As Long
Dim strWriteBuffer As String * 256
Dim lngBytesWritten As Long
Dim strReadBuffer As String * 256
```

```
Dim lngBytesRead As Long
Dim lngTotalBytesRead As Long
Dim strLoggerBuffer As String
Dim flFailed As Boolean
Dim flTimedout As Boolean
Dim flFatalError As Boolean
Dim ftStatus As Long
```

The next section opens the device and checks whether the step has been successful. The variables that are to be written to the device are then loaded prior to being written to the device. This is then followed by another error checking process.

```
'Open device
If FT_Open(0, lngHandle) <> FT_OK Then
   Exit Sub
End If

'Load write variables
strWriteBuffer = (a$)
lngBytesWritten = 0

'Write output
If FT_Write(lngHandle, strWriteBuffer, Len(strWriteBuffer),
lngBytesWritten) <> FT_OK Then
   xit = FT_Close(lngHandle)
   Exit Sub
End If
```

The read process is preceded by the setting of a number of variables prior to the actual process itself. It will be seen that the read is encased in a *Do....While* loop which, coupled with error checking, ensures that all the data to be read is accumulated. The read data is placed in the variable a$.

```
'Load read variables
flTimedout = False
flFatalError = False

lngTotalBytesRead = 0
lngBytesRead = 0
readsize = 1
lngTotalBytesRead = 0

Do
lngBytesRead = 0
'Read input
 ftStatus = FT_Read(lngHandle, strReadBuffer, readsize -
lngTotalBytesRead, lngBytesRead)

'Check for success of read
If (ftStatus = FT_OK) Or (ftStatus = FT_IO_ERROR) Then
   If lngBytesRead > 0 Then
   strLoggerBuffer = strLoggerBuffer + Left(strReadBuffer,
lngBytesRead)
   lngTotalBytesRead = lngTotalBytesRead + lngBytesRead
   Else
      flTimedout = True
```

```
   End If
Else
   flFatalError = True
End If
Loop Until (lngTotalBytesRead = readsize) Or (flTimedout = True) Or
(flFatalError = True)
'Display input data or reason for failure
If (flTimedout = False) And (flFatalError = False) Then
   a$ = Asc((strReadBuffer))
End If
```

To complete the Readprog routine the device is closed.

```
'Close device
 xit = FT_Close(lngHandle)
End Sub
```

Writeprog

The features of the Writeprog have already been described above. The device is opened, the variable is written to the device and the device is then closed. At each stage the process is checked for success.

```
'Write port routine
Public Sub Writeprog()
'Open device
If FT_Open(0, lngHandle) <> FT_OK Then
   Exit Sub
End If
'Load write variables
strWriteBuffer = (a$)
```

```
lngBytesWritten = 0

'Write output
If FT_Write(lngHandle, strWriteBuffer, Len(strWriteBuffer), lngBytesWritten) <> FT_OK Then
   xit = FT_Close(lngHandle)
   Exit Sub
End If

'Close device
xit = FT_Close(lngHandle)

End Sub
```

PortOut

It can be seen from the Readprog and Writeprog routines that a number of parameters are required for the Read and Write functions. This can be reduced by producing specific functions which only contain the essential information.

The syntax required for using PortOut is:

PortO=PortOut(Reg,OUT%)

As the USB I/O 24 module is mimicking the 8255A PPI, Reg refers to the Port address that is to be used and OUT% is data between 0 and 255 that is to be transmitted. A Case structure is used to make the programming as compact as possible. Case 0, 1 and 2 refer to data being transmitted out of Ports A, B and C respectively.

```
'Writing data function
Public Function PortOut(Reg, OUT%)
'Output data
Select Case Reg
'Port A
Case 0
a$ = "A" + Chr$(OUT%)
Writeprog
'Port B
Case 1
a$ = "B" + Chr$(OUT%)
Writeprog
'Port C
Case 2
a$ = "C" + Chr$(OUT%)
Writeprog
```

In Case 3 Reg is accessing the Control Register which is used to determine the direction of data flow. OUT% now refers to the Code column of Table 2.3.

If the Outputs are replaced by logic 0 and the Inputs by logic 1, Table 2.3 can be converted into Table 3.1.

	Active	Port A	Port C (Upper)	Port B	Port C (Lower)	Code (decimal)
Weighting	128	16	8	2	1	Total
	1	0	0	0	0	128
	1	0	0	0	1	129
	1	0	0	1	0	130
	1	0	0	1	1	131
	1	0	1	0	0	136
	1	0	1	0	1	137
	1	0	1	1	0	138
	1	0	1	1	1	139
	1	1	0	0	0	144
	1	1	0	0	1	145
	1	1	0	1	0	146
	1	1	0	1	1	147
	1	1	1	0	0	152
	1	1	1	0	1	153
	1	1	1	1	0	154
	1	1	1	1	1	155

Table 3.1 8255A control word code settings

The settings of Port A, Port B, Port C(Hi) and Port C (Lo) will produce a decimal code after taking into account the weightings of each column.

The code has to initially take the decimal code and create the binary equivalent.

```
Case 3
'Control Register - set Ports A, B & C directions (use register codes)
Dim M(8) As Integer
z% = OUT%
'Convert OUT% into binary format
For i = 0 To 7
x% = Int(z% / 2)
M(i) = (z% - 2 * x%)
z% = x%
Next
```

Bits 4 and 1 store the direction of Port A and B respectively.

```
'Set Port A direction
If M(4) = 0 Then
a$ = "!A" + Chr$(0)
Else
a$ = "!A" + Chr$(255)
End If
Writeprog
'Set Port B direction
If M(1) = 0 Then
a$ = "!B" + Chr$(0)
Else
a$ = "!B" + Chr$(255)
End If
Writeprog
```

Bits 3 and 0 hold the states of the Upper and Lower parts of Port C which must be concatenated to create the Port C direction.

```
'Allocate Port C(Hi) direction
If M(3) = 0 Then
w% = 0
Else
w% = 240
End If
'Allocate Port C(Lo) direction
```

```
If M(0) = 0 Then
w% = 0 + w%
Else
w% = 15 + w%
End If
'Set Port C direction
a$ = "!C" + Chr$(w%)
Writeprog
End Select
End Function
```

PortIn

The PortIn function is used to read data in from a particular Port of the USB I/O 24 module. The syntax is:

inp% = PortIn (Reg)

Reg is the Port address that is being accessed and inp% is the data between 0 and 255 which is being returned. Again a Case structure is used with Case equalling 0, 1 and 2 corresponding to Ports A, B and C, and the result being placed into inp%

```
'Reading data function
Public Function PortIn(Reg) As Variant
'Input data
Select Case Reg
'Port A
Case 0
a$ = "a"
Readprog
Case 1
```

```
a$ = "b"
Readprog
Case 2
a$ = "c"
Readprog
End Select
'Get data
PortIn = Val(a$)
inp% = PortIn
End Function
```

Summary

The io_usb.bas file is used in all of the Visual Basic projects that are going to be produced in future chapters. It provides all the reference material that is needed to write and read data to and from the USB I/O 24 module.

The relevant functions to be called from FTD2XX.DLL are initially declared. The writing and reading to the device has been shown clearly in all its code and finally two user-friendly read and write functions have been introduced.

The code that you have written is involved, and typing mistakes are easy to make. The next stage is to write a simple project to use io_usb.bas and to rectify any errors before using it in more complex circumstances.

4

Digital Input/Output

Using the USB I/O 24 module

The next phase in the development of the use of the USB I/O 24 module is to check that it works. This will involve using an interface board called the User Port Tester which will monitor the state of the two Ports A and B plus their associated control lines. Two programs will then be developed. One will check the output capabilities of the module and the other the input. These two programs are important since they will always come in useful later to check that the system is working. In any interface situation there are several items that have to work, i.e. the interface module, the interface board, the connecting cable and the software. Any one of these items may have a fault and it is always useful to revert back to well-tried and tested equipment and software.

Interface Boards

The programs used in the subsequent chapters use interface boards which are connected to the USB I/O 24 module. Details of the interface boards can be found in the Appendix. Each interface board has a 20-way IDC ribbon cable connector plug which connects to the ribbon cable from the USB I/O 24 module.

The interface boards are:

i. **User Port Tester** – a board to monitor input and output data of the USB I/O 24 module.

ii. **Stepper** – a board to vary the speed of a stepper motor.

iii. **8DAC** – an 8-bit digital to analogue converter which is capable of producing voltage outputs in the ranges 0 to +5.10V and –2.56V to +2.54V.

iv. **8ADC** – an 8-bit successive approximation analogue to digital converter which can convert voltage inputs of between 0 and +5.10V with a resolution of 2mV and between –5.12 and +5.10V with a resolution of 4mV

v. **12ADC** – a 12-bit dual ramp integrating analogue to digital converter which can convert voltages between –4.095V and +4.095V with a resolution of 1mV. Using an instrumentation pre-amplifier it is possible to obtain additional resolutions of 1μV, 10μV and 100μV.

The Appendix provides details of each board, the PCB design, a component overlay and a list of components required to make up the board. The boards can be assembled by any person who has some knowledge of electronic circuit construction.

If it is not possible to use the interface boards, the reader should find sufficient detail in the programs such that the techniques can be used in other applications.

The User Port Tester board

This is a board which can be connected to either Port A or Port B plus the appropriate parts of Port C of the USB I/O 24 module. It is used to test input and output programs of the USB I/O 24 module card. The states of the data lines connected to the computer are set by the USB I/O 24 module and are indicated by a 10 LED bar display (Figure 4.1).

In order to understand how the USB I/O 24 module can be used, its operation will be introduced by referring to examples written in Visual Basic. Data can be transmitted to and from the User Port Tester board using the Visual Basic functions PortOut and PortIn that have been introduced in Chapter 3.

A program to achieve this requires the following steps:

1) Initialisation - set up the USB I/O 24 module ports as inputs or outputs
2) Read or write data through the desired ports A, B or C.

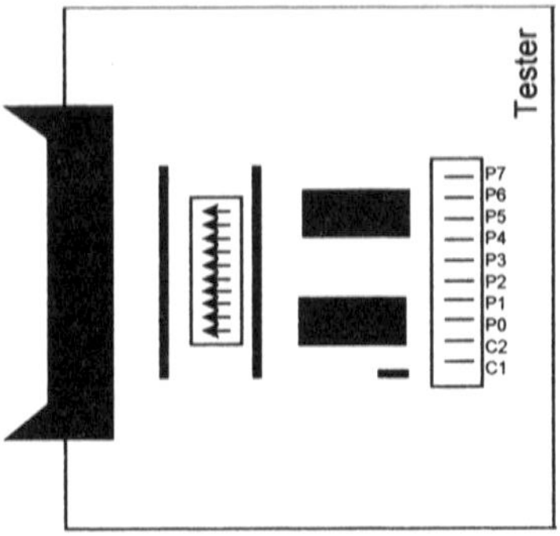

Figure 4.1 The User Port Tester board

Creating a User Port Tester Input Form

This program produces a User Port Tester Input Form to read data fed from the User Port Tester board to the USB I/O 24 module connected to the PC.

On the Visual Basic Form, input data is plotted on a graph in a Picture Box. The Form should have the layout shown in Figure 4.2. and consists of one Label Box *Data Recorded*, one Text box and a Command Button. The lower part of the Form contains a Picture Box with two Label boxes (*Voltage* and *Time*) placed as shown.

The Caption on the Form is *Input*.

The code associated with the various items is listed below.

The Declarations

This assigns the addresses to the Ports A, B and C and also the control register. To make the program as versatile as possible the addresses of the registers are referenced to REGA. This means that should the program be used in the future with a commercial I/O plug-in card, only the base address of Port A will need to be altered.

The Declarations also make the control register variable *out%* Private.

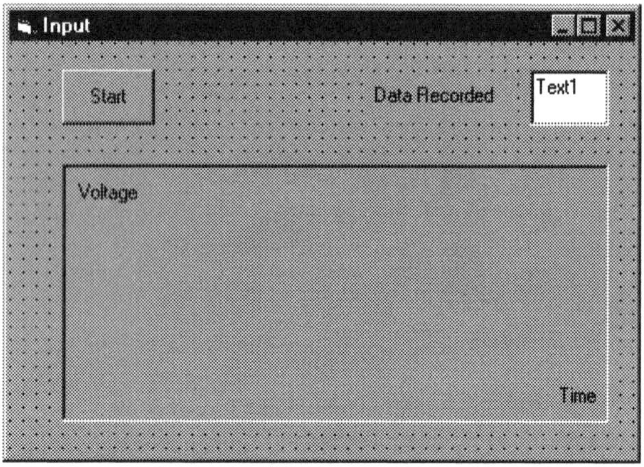

Figure 4.2 Layout of the User Port Tester Input Form

```
'Declare parameters
Const REGA = 0
Const REGB = REGA + 1
Const REGC = REGA + 2
Const CREG = REGA + 3
Private out%
```

The Form

This configures the USB I/O 24 module and initialises the input Text boxes.

```
Private Sub Form_Load()
'Assign control register code
out% = 155
'Configure port as input
```

```
PortO = PortOut(CREG, out%)
'Display input value
Text1.Text = ""
End Sub
```

The function which accesses the DLL to output data to the USB I/O 24 module is:

PortO = PortOut(CREG, out%)

This feeds the data *out%* to the register address CREG. The dummy return value, 1, is assigned to the variable *PortO* which is never used. *out%* must have a value assigned to it before the procedure is called.

The Command button

The function of the Command Button is to initiate the input of data from the User Port Tester board and plot it on the Picture Box. Whilst the data is being plotted the caption on the button changes from *Start* to *Plotting*. Initially the axes are drawn bearing in mind that the origin (0,0) is at the top left-hand corner of the Picture Box.

Once the plotting starts, the *DoEvents()* statement is required to break in and stop the program. The function of this statement is to revert the program to the Windows operating system and initiate an interrupt process. 200 data points are plotted.

```
Private Sub Command1_Click()
'Change Start button To Plotting
Command1.Caption = "Plotting"
'Clear picture box
Picture1.Cls
'Calibrate picture box
Picture1.Scale (-50, -50)-(250, 300)
```

```
'Draw horizontal axis
Picture1.Line (0, 255)-(200, 255)
'Draw vertical axis
Picture1.Line (0, 0)-(0, 255)
'Goto origin
Picture1.PSet (0, 255)
'Plot 200 points
For I = 1 To 200
'Read Port
inp% = PortIn(REGA)
'Redirect to operating system
t = DoEvents()
'Display input readings
Text1.Text = INP%
'Plot input readings
Picture1.Line -(I, 255 - INP%)
'Delay
For n = 1 To 1000000
Next n
Next I
'Start button reverts to stop status
Command1.Caption = "Start"
End Sub
```

The other BASIC command which accesses the DLL is:

inp%=PortIn(REGA)

This reads register REGA and the returned value is assigned to the variable inp%.

The Userin program

Form1 is saved as userin.frm and the io_usb.bas module should be added to the project. Check in the project window that this has been done. The files should be as shown in Table 4.1.

Project	Project1 (userin.vbp)
Form	Form1 (userin.frm)
module	module1 (io_usb.bas)

Table 4.1 The userin.vbp project files

Running the Userin program

When the program is run Form1 will appear. Pressing the Start button will initiate the plotting routine. The switches on the User Port Tester board can be changed and the input to the USB I/O 24 module board monitored both on the graph and in the *Data Recorded* text box. Figure 4.4 shows a typical set of results. The rate of data acquisition is dependent upon the delay and this can be varied by the *For n = 1 To 1000000* statement in the above program.

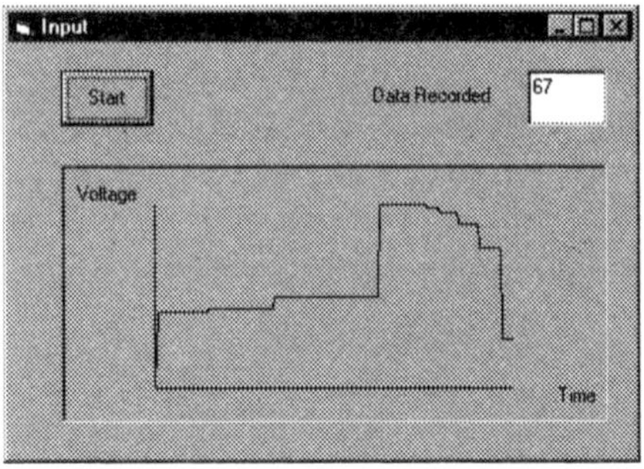

Figure 4.4. Userin.vbp in operation

Exercise 4.1

4.1.1 Check that the program works and then rem out the statement *t=DoEvents()* in the Command button procedure.

Does the program always now respond to a *Break* key press?

Creating a User Port Tester Output Form

This program produces a User Port Tester Output Form to feed data out from the PC into the USB I/O 24 module.

Data is generated using a Scroll Bar on the Visual Basic Form. The *Max* value in the Properties Windows of the Scroll bar is set to 255 (Figure 4.5).

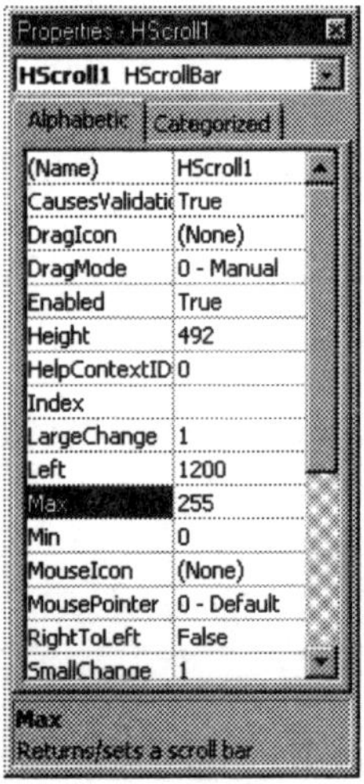

Figure 4.5 The Scroll bar Property Window

The Form should have the layout shown in Figure 4.6. and consists of one Label Box (*Output Signal*), one Text box and a horizontal scroll bar. The Caption on the Form is *Output*.

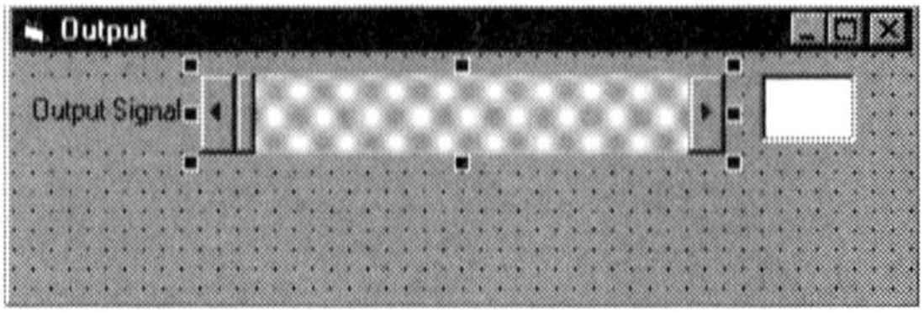

Figure 4.6 Layout of the User Port Tester Output Form

The code associated with the various items is listed below.

The Declarations

This is identical to the Declarations made in the Userin.frm program.

```
'Declare parameters
Const REGA = 0
Const REGB = REGA + 1
Const REGC = REGA + 2
Const CREG = REGA + 3
Private out%
```

The Form

This reads the setting of the Scroll bar, configures the USB I/O 24 module and initialises the output Text box.

```
Private Sub Form_Load()
'Assign control register code
out% = 128
'Configure port as output
PortO = PortOut(CREG, out%)
'Read output value from scroll bar
output% = HScroll1.Value
```

```
'Display output value
Text1.Text = output%
'Send output value to port
PortO = PortOut(REGA, output%)
End Sub
```

out% is set to a value which is used to configure Ports A and B as outputs.

The Scroll bar is then read and its value is then outputted to Port A.

The Scroll bar

This procedure enables the USB I/O 24 module to output data, which is displayed on the LEDs on the User Port Tester board. The data is changed by moving the setting of the scroll bar. This can vary from 0 to 255.

```
Private Sub HScroll1_Change()
'Configure port as output
PortO = PortOut(CREG, out%)
'Read output value from scroll bar
output% = HScroll1.Value
'Display output value
Text1.Text = output%
'Send output value to port
PortO = PortOut(REGA, output%)
End Sub
```

The Userout program

Form1 should be saved as userout.Frm and the io_usb.bas module should be added to the project. Check in the project window that this has been done. The files should be as shown in Table 4.2.

Project	Project1 (userout.vbp)
Form	Form1 (userout.frm)
module	module1 (io_usb.bas)

Table 4.2 The userout.vbp project files

Running the Userout program

The program will start immediately it is set running. The mouse is used to move the Scroll bar up and down the scale. The output reading is displayed in decimal format in the Text box and in binary form on the User Port Tester LEDs. Figure 4.8 shows the Form when the program is running.

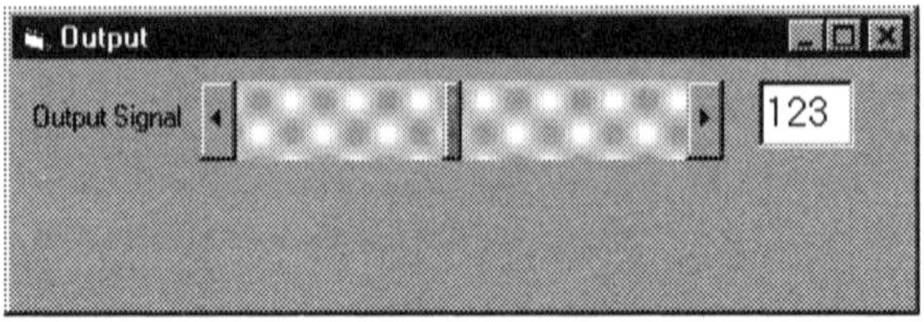

Figure 4.8 The userout.vbp project running

Exercise 4.2

4.2.1 Write a program which sets ports A, B and C as outputs and operating in a loop causes the lights in the bar code display to light up in sequence, moving back and forth across the 10 bars.

Modify the Form to have a bar display which is illuminated in a similar manner.

4.2.2 Extend the above program so that two LEDs light up in sequence, move in opposite directions across the bar display from either end and appear to cross over. Again use all ten LEDs.

Summary

Once you have these two programs running successfully you will have managed to get data in and out of the USB I/O 24 module. The following chapters will now utilise these features and they will show you how easy PC interfacing can be.

5

Stepper Motors

Stepper motor applications

Stepper motors may be used in many applications in the laboratory. They can be used in situations where accurate positioning is required, in automatic machinery and robotics, and where there is a requirement for continuous motion which can be controlled by a computer. Stepper motors are available with a wide range of power and torque ratings to suit a number of applications.

What is a stepper motor?

A simple stepper motor can be described as a permanent magnet (the rotor) which is free to rotate about an axis, and 4 coils located at equal positions around the rotor. Current can be passed through the coils so that magnetic fields are created and the rotor attempts to align with these fields.

The permanent magnet, the variable reluctance stepper motor and hybrids of the two are more commonly available commercially because their design enables smaller step angles to be obtained with higher precision. The Stepper driver board is designed to drive a 4-phase stepper motor which has 4 coils (i.e. phases) and is the most common type available. The 4 coils are aligned at 90 degrees to each other and the direction of the magnetic field produced by each coil alone is shown in Figure 5.1.

The permanent magnet rotor will line up with the resultant magnetic field so that as the coils are energised in cyclic order, rotation of the rotor will be produced. In the full-step mode it is usual to energise 2 adjacent coils at once since this will produce more torque and power. Thus the coils are energised in the sequence given in Table 5.1, which rotates the rotor to the positions shown. To produce counter-clockwise rotation the coils are energised in reverse order.

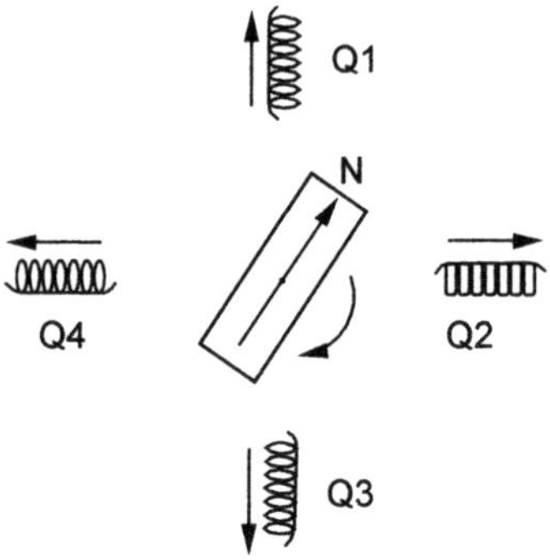

Figure 5.1 Permanent magnet stepper motor

Step No	Q1	Q2	Q3	Q4	Decimal	Field direction
1	1	1	0	0	3	↗
2	0	1	1	0	6	↘
3	0	0	1	1	12	↙
4	1	0	0	1	9	↖

Table 5.1 Full-step mode, order in which coils are energised

In the half-step mode the coils are energised in the sequence which sweeps the magnetic field and hence the rotor to the positions given in Table 5.2.

Step No	Q1	Q2	Q3	Q4	Decimal	Field direction
1	1	1	0	0	3	↗
2	0	1	0	0	2	→
3	0	1	1	0	6	↘
4	0	0	1	0	4	↓
5	0	0	1	1	12	↙
6	0	0	0	1	8	←
7	1	0	0	1	9	↖
8	1	0	0	0	1	↑

Table 5.2 Half-step mode, order in which coils are energised

The Stepper Board

The Stepper board is used to directly drive the coils and has been designed to drive two stepper motors. As the PC cannot provide sufficient current for the coils of the motor, a laboratory power supply is used to supply 5V between the supply and ground terminals of the Stepper board.

Figure 5.2 shows the layout of the Stepper board.

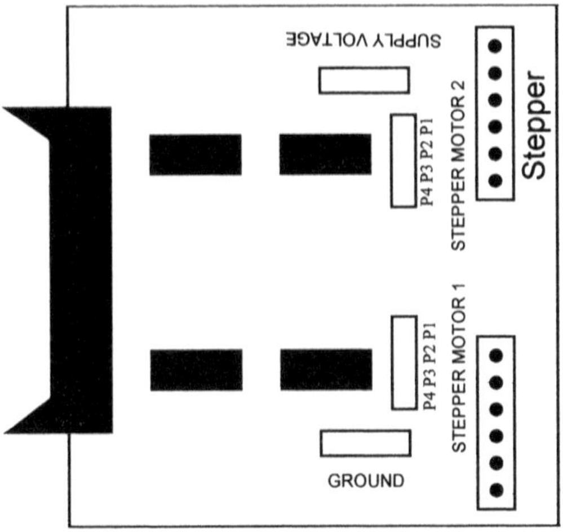

Figure 5.2 Layout of the Stepper board

Figure 5.3 shows how the board is connected to the PC and to the stepper motor. A power supply is required to provide sufficient current for the motor coils, usually between 0.5A and 1.0A. The leads from the motor are plugged into the stepper board.

Stepper motors are used for many different applications and a good source of ones suitable for this application is the motor out of an old disc drive.

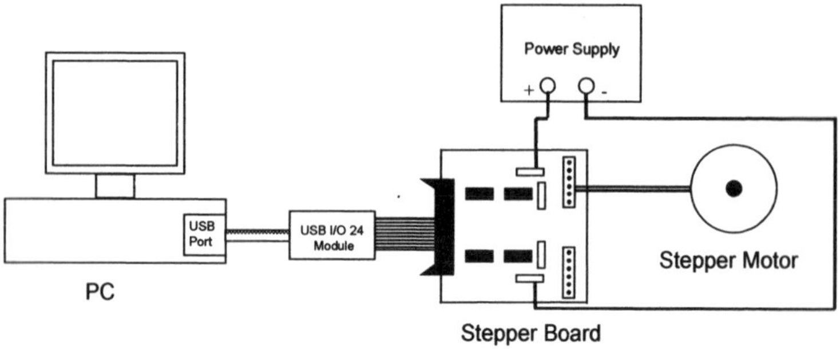

Figure 5.3 Stepper motor connections to the Stepper board

Determining the stepper motor code

Sometimes the code for a stepper motor is unavailable and it is necessary to run a short program to find the code and also check the leads of the motor. Figure 5.4 shows how the leads of a stepper motor are connected.

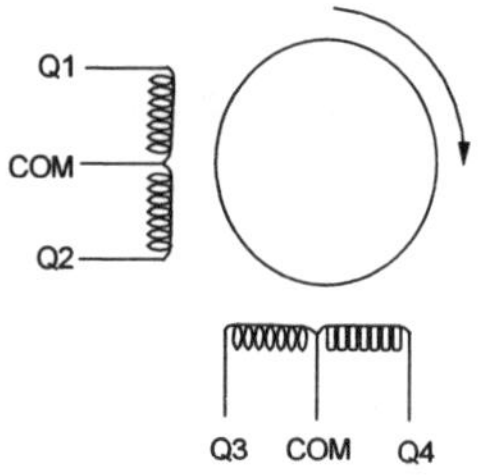

Figure 5.4 Connections to a stepper motor

There are normally six leads from the motor. Two are common and are connected to ground (0V), the other four are connected to Q1, Q2, Q3 and Q4. These should be connected to P1, P2, P3 and P4 on the stepper board.

The motor code can be found by applying signals to the motor and finding which combination will cause the motor to rotate. Using Visual Basic this can be easily achieved by modifying the userout.vbp project used in the previous chapter.

Connect up the Stepper board, stepper motor and power supply as shown in Figure 5.3 and start up userout.vbp.

The main modification to the Form is to add a Command button with the caption *Send*. Figure 5.5 shows the appearance of the Form.

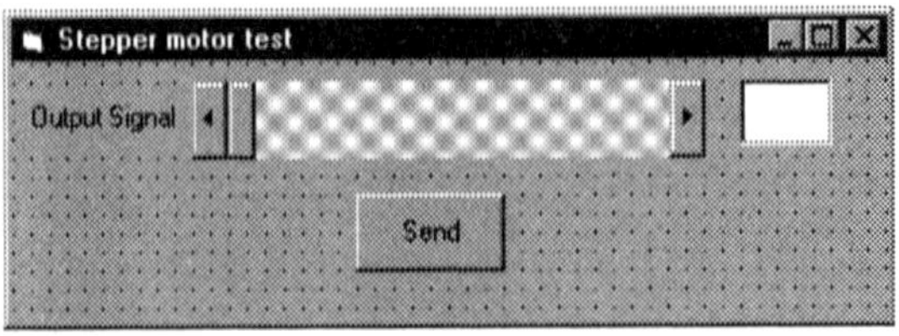

Figure 5.5 The stepper motor test Form

The Caption on the Form is changed to *Stepper motor test* and the *Max* property of HScroll1 is changed to 15.

The code required is:

Declarations

This is the declaration of the USB I/O 24 module addresses and the parameter *output%* which may be found under Private.

```
'Declare parameters
Const REGA = 0
Const REGB = REGA + 1
Const REGC = REGA + 2
Const CREG = REGA + 3
Private output%
```

Command button - Send

Only one value at a time is sent to the USB I/O 24 module.

```
Private Sub Command1_Click()
'Send output value to port
PortO = PortOut(REGA, output%)
End Sub
```

The Form

This is similar to the userout.frm routine.

```
Private Sub Form_Load()
'Assign control register code
out% = 128
'Configure port as output
PortO = PortOut(CREG, out%)
'Read output value from scroll bar
output% = HScroll1.Value
'Display output value
Text1.Text = output%
'Send output value to port
PortO = PortOut(REGA, output%)
End Sub
```

Scroll bar

Again very similar to the userout.frm but without the transmission of the data statement.

```
Private Sub HScroll1_Change()
'Read output value from scroll bar
output% = HScroll1.Value
'Display output value
Text1.Text = output%
End Sub
```

Steptest.vbp Project

The Form should be saved as steptest.frm, the module io_usb.bas added and the project saved as steptest.vbp. The files should be as shown in Table 5.3.

Project	Project1 (steptest.vbp)
Form	Form1 (steptest.frm)
module	module1 (io_usb.bas)

Table 5.3 The steptest.vbp project files

Using the Steptest program

When the program is run the user should send separate values to the stepper board. A check should be made to see if the rotor of the motor moves. It should be possible to find a sequence of values which cause the rotor to rotate smoothly. This code sequence can then be used in the next experiment.

Variable speed stepper motor

This program is designed to simply start a stepper motor and enable the user to select a suitable speed of rotation. Initially it is necessary to configure all of the pins on the USB I/O 24 module to be outputs and then to write the correct code so that the rotor of the stepper motor is energised in the appropriate manner. Time has to be allowed for the rotor to reach its new position so that there have to be suitable time delays between energising each of the coils - this is achieved using delay loops.

In the experiment described below, the Stepper is connected to Port A of the USB I/O 24 module and the motor is connected to Connection 1 on the Stepper board.

The Form

Start up Visual Basic and select **File** and **New Project**. Place on the Form a Horizontal Scroll Bar, a Timer and a Text box as shown in Figure 5.7.

Set the Interval property of Timer1 to 1000.

The Max property of the Horizontal Scroll Bar should be set to 100.

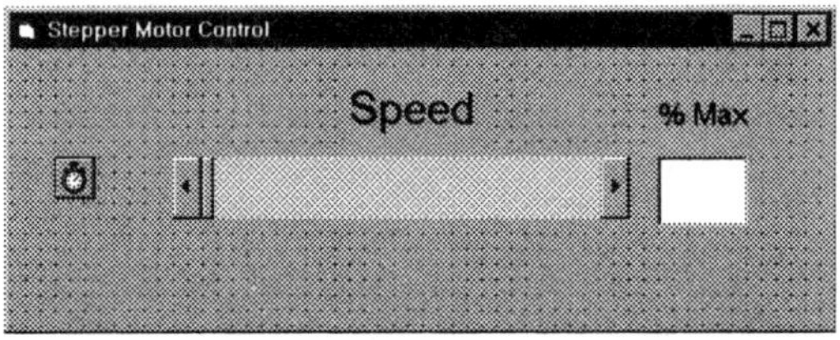

Figure 5.7 Stepper Motor Control Form

Add Labels above the Scroll bar and the Text box and change the Captions to *Speed* and *%Max* respectively. Also change the Caption of the Form to *Stepper Motor Control.*

The Code

The basis of the control of the stepper motor is via the Timer1 control. Each time the Timer1 control is called the stepper motor is permitted to move. The frequency with which this occurs is controlled by the Timer1 *Interval* property. It is this property that the user changes with the Scroll bar.

Declarations

This sets up the USB I/O 24 module registers.

```
'Declare parameters
Const REGA = 0
Const REGB = REGA + 1
Const REGC = REGA + 2
Const CREG = REGA + 3
```

The Form

This sets up the variables for the USB I/O 24 module, reads the Scroll bar value and places it in the Text box and switches off Timer1. This ensures the *Stepper* routine is not called and the stepper motor does not move.

```
Private Sub Form_Load()
'Display scroll bar setting
Text1.Text = HScroll1.Value
'Switch off Timer1
Timer1.Enabled = False
End Sub
```

The Scroll Bar

This enables the user to set the speed of the stepper motor. The setting of the scroll bar is read as a percentage of the maximum speed and then converted into a value which is placed into the interval property of Timer1. Timer1 is then enabled so that the Stepper routine is regularly called

```
Private Sub HScroll1_Change()
'Display scroll bar setting
Text1.Text = HScroll1.Value
'Assign scroll bar setting to variable
scrolltime = HScroll1.Value
'Determine Timer1 interval setting
Timer1.Interval = (1000 - scrolltime * 1000 / 100) + 1
'Switch off Timer1 when scroll bar setting is zero
If Timer1.Interval = 1001 Then
Timer1.Enabled = False
Else
```

```
Timer1.Enabled = True
End If
End Sub
```

The Timer

This calls the Stepper routine at the set intervals.

```
Private Sub Timer1_Timer()
'Call stepper routine
Stepper
End Sub
```

The Stepper routine

Use the **Tools/Add Procedure** menu to create this routine which will appear in the General section of the program. Its function is to configure the USB I/O 24 module as an output and then output the relevant code to the coils so that they can be energised in the correct order.

```
Private Sub Stepper()
'Assign stepper motor parameters (Insert code for your motor here)
N1 = 3: N2 = 6: N3 = 12: N4 = 9
'Assign control register code
cregout% = 128
'Configure port as output
PortO = PortOut(CREG, cregout%)
'Send out stepper motor parameter
PortO = PortOut(REGA, N1)
'Delay (alter according to PC speed)
For I = 1 To 100000: Next I
```

```
'Send out stepper motor parameter
PortO = PortOut(REGA, N2)
'Delay (alter according to PC speed)
For I = 1 To 100000: Next I
'Send out stepper motor parameter
PortO = PortOut(REGA, N3)
'Delay (alter according to PC speed)
For I = 1 To 100000: Next I
'Send out stepper motor parameter
PortO = PortOut(REGA, N4)
'Delay (alter according to PC speed)
For I = 1 To 100000: Next I
End Sub
```

The step.vbp

The program is saved as step.frm. io_usb.bas is added to the project which is then saved as step.vbp. The files should be as shown in Table 5.4.

Project	Project1 (step.vbp)
Form	Form1 (step.frm)
module	module1 (io_usb.bas)

Table 5.4 The step.vbp project files

Running the program

The stepper motor does not initially move when the program is first run. As soon as the scroll bar is moved the motor will rotate and the speed will increase as the scroll bar is moved further to the right. If it is taken back to the origin the motor will stop.

Exercise 5

5.1 Modify the program so that the motor can rotate either clockwise or counter-clockwise.

5.2 Add a separate stop/start command button.

5.3 Use Table 5.2 to modify the program so that coils are energised in the half-step mode.

5.4 Assume that the stepper motor is used to wind a lift-car up and down a shaft.

If the number of revolutions to move the lift-car from one floor to the next is 20 and the number of floors including the basement is 6, write a program that will enable the lift-car to move up or down to any desired floor.

Modify the program so that:

a) users on the top and ground floor have priority

b) an emergency button on the Form stops the lift-car.

Summary

A stepper motor is controlled by sending out a series of numbers in a repetitive manner. The major problem is getting the correct sequence of numbers and you now have a program to deduce those numbers.

In addition you have developed a program that controls the speed of a stepper motor and are aware of the problems that are encountered with varying the speed of a motor and ensuring that the rotor moves cleanly from one step to the next.

6

DAC

Digital to Analogue Conversion

A digital to analogue converter is a device which produces an analogue output, i.e. a current or voltage, when a digital input is applied to it. There are two basic forms that are available. One is the weighted resistor DAC and the other is the R-2R ladder DAC. Selecting suitably matched resistors makes the construction of the former very difficult and so it is not often used in modern DACs. Nevertheless the theory of it will be found in many electronics textbooks, e.g. *Data Converters* by G B Clayton. The R-2R ladder DAC is very common and is the basis of the device used in the 8DAC board which is used in this chapter.

Theory of the R-2R ladder DAC

The R-2R ladder is an arrangement of resistors that produces an analogue output which is proportional to the digital bit pattern which is applied to it. Figure 6.1 shows how the series resistors R and the shunt resistors 2R are connected for a 3-bit DAC.

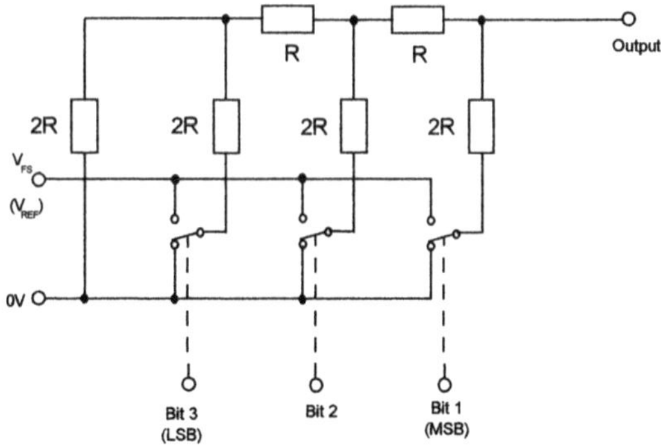

Figure 6.1 R-2R ladder DAC circuit

The bottom of each shunt resistor has a single-pole double-throw electronic switch which connects the resistor to ground or to the reference voltage source.

The output voltage is given by:

$$V_0 = \left(\frac{V_1}{2}\right) + \left(\frac{V_2}{4}\right) + \left(\frac{V_3}{8}\right)$$

where V_1= 0V or V_{ref}, V_2= 0V or V_{ref}, V_3= 0V or V_{ref}.

This design of DAC has many advantages in that only two values of resistors are required and these can be trimmed and matched during the manufacture of the DAC integrated circuit. In addition the resistors are mounted on the same substrate so that all experience identical temperature fluctuations. This type of DAC is referred to as a multiplying DAC, which means that the output voltage is proportional to the reference voltage. Hence if the value of the reference voltage is altered, the range of the corresponding output will also change. The 8DAC board has an 8-bit resolution so that the 3-rung ladder shown in Figure 6.1 is extended to 8 rungs.

Unipolar and Bipolar

The smallest quanta of output that the DAC can produce depends upon the LSB (Least Significant Bit). A factor which affects the size of the LSB is whether the analogue range is entirely positive (unipolar) or both negative and positive (bipolar). The maximum value of the output is denoted by the term FS (Full Scale). In bipolar mode the minimum value is referred to as -FS.

In the case of the unipolar 8-bit DAC with a nominal 5.12V output, the corresponding digital inputs and analogue outputs are given in Table 6.1.

	Binary Input	Analogue Output
+FS - 1LSB	1111 1111	+5.10V
1 LSB	0000 0001	+0.02V
0	0000 0000	0V

Table 6.1 Unipolar 8-bit DAC output

If the output range is bipolar with a nominal range of ±2.56V, the digital inputs and corresponding analogue outputs are shown in Table 6.2.

	Binary Input	Analogue Output
+FS - 1 LSB	1111 1111	+2.54V
1 LSB	1000 0001	+0.02V
0	1000 0000	0V
-1LSB	0111 1111	-0.02V
-FS	0000 0000	-2.56V

Table 6.2 Bipolar 8-bit DAC output

If the Tables 6.1 and 6.2 are compared it can be seen that the extent of the voltage ranges are identical, though the bipolar range is centred about 0V and the maximum positive voltage is half that of the unipolar value. Also the leading or most significant bit (MSB) in the bipolar mode is used to indicate the polarity of the analogue signal, i.e. 0 denotes negative, 1 is positive.

Using the 8DAC board

The USB I/O 24 module provides two ports to which the DAC board may be connected. Each port consists of 8 data lines which can be set up as either inputs or outputs plus two control lines which are used as interrupt or pulse lines. These ports must be configured so that digital data can be transmitted to the 8DAC board. The digital data is latched into the DAC so that the analogue output will remain constant even when the DAC is not being addressed by the PC.

The program steps are as follows:

1. Configure the port	Sets the data lines as outputs and initialises the control lines.
2. Control line 2 low	Sets the WR line low so that the DAC responds to data activity on the data bus.
3. Apply data to the port	Takes the data and places it at the input of the DAC.
4. Control line 2 high	WR goes high to latch data into DAC.

Configuring the port

Two registers are used to set up the port.

a) Input/output register

b) Control register

In addition control line 2 is connected to the WR line of the DAC. This line is taken low to access the DAC and high to latch the data.

Features of the 8DAC board

The 8DAC is a voltage output 8-bit digital to analogue converter (DAC) board based upon the AD7524 8-bit multiplying digital to analogue converter (Figure 6.2).

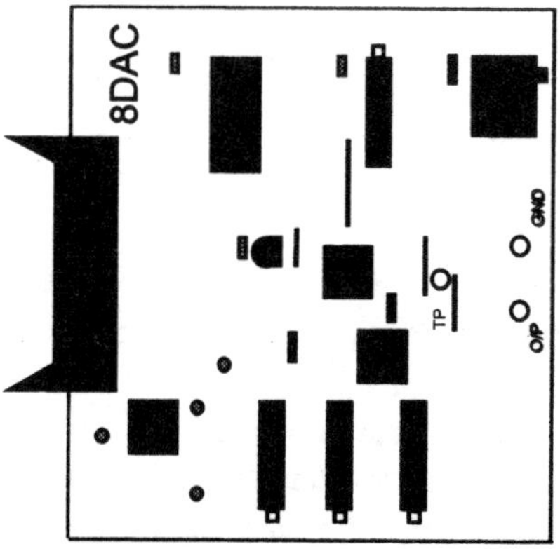

Figure 6.2 The 8DAC board

The board connects to the USB I/O 24 module which is attached to the USB port of the PC. The 8DAC board can be used in either the unipolar (positive only output) or bipolar mode (positive and negative output) with a resolution of 255 steps between the maximum and minimum voltage outputs. The board is powered from the internal power supply of the PC. It is possible to obtain a full-scale range (FSR) of the voltage output up to a maximum of +5.12V in the unipolar mode. The selection of the DAC polarity mode is made using the on-board switch.

The Program

The configuration and output of data to the 8DAC can be reduced to two statements which can be easily handled by Visual Basic through the control register and Port A of the USB I/O 24 module.

Start up Visual Basic and select **New Project** from the **File** menu.

The Form

Figure 6.3 shows the layout of the DAC Form.

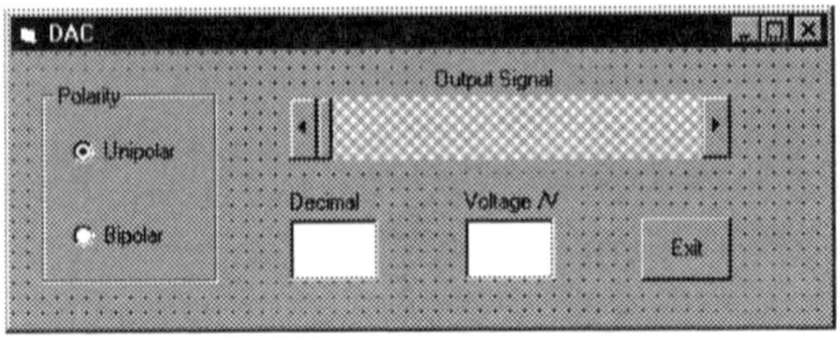

Figure 6.3 The DAC Form

Place on the Form a Frame with a caption Polarity, a Horizontal Scroll bar and two Text boxes. Place two Option buttons into the Polarity frame. Insert three Label boxes with captions *Output Signal*, Decimal and *Voltage /V*. Also add a Command Button with a caption of *Exit*.

In the Properties window of the Option1 button, change *Visible* to *True*. This ensures that the Unipolar option appears active when the program starts up.

The *Max* property of the Scroll bar should be changed to 255.

The Code

The code can now be assigned to the controls.

The Option Buttons

These are used in conjunction with the 8DAC board to select whether the output from the DAC should be unipolar or bipolar. The current setting of the scroll bar is converted into the appropriate Voltage scale and the DAC will follow the change.

```
Private Sub Option1_Click()
'Set Polarity flag to Unipolar
Polarity = 0
'Goto display routine
display
End Sub
```

```
Private Sub Option2_Click()
'Set Polarity flag to Bipolar
Polarity = 1
'Goto display routine
display
End Sub
```

The Scroll Bar

This is used to change the value of the DAC output. The setting of the scroll bar is displayed in Text box 1.

```
Private Sub HScroll1_Change()
'assign scroll bar setting to variable
inval = HScroll1.Value
```

```
'Output setting to DAC
PortO = PortOut(REGA, inval)
'Goto display routine
display
End Sub
```

The Form

The interface board is configured as output for Ports A and B. The DAC is set to the current value of the scroll bar. This value in decimal form appears in Text box 1 and the voltage notation is in Text box 2.

```
Private Sub Form_Load()
'Select Port A as output
out% = 128
'Configure USB  I/O 24 module
PortO = PortOut(CREG, out%)
'Zero DAC output setting
inval = 0
'set Polarity to Unipolar
Polarity = 0
'Goto Display
display
End Sub
```

The Display Procedure

This takes the setting of the scroll bar and converts it into the equivalent voltage based upon the polarity set on the DAC. The procedure also enables the DAC on Port A of the USB I/O 24 module, outputs a value to the DAC and then latches the data into the DAC.

The procedure can be created by typing in *Private Sub Display ()* upon which the procedure is then automatically created. Alternatively the **Tools/Add Procedure** menus can be used and the *Private* option selected.

```
Private Sub display()
'Select equivalent voltage settings
If Polarity = 0 Then
Invalvolt = (5.12 * inval) / 256
Else
Invalvolt = (inval - 128) * 2.56 / 128
End If
'Enable DAC for new data
PortO = PortOut(REGC, 0)
'Send output scroll bar setting to DAC
PortO = PortOut(REGA, inval)
'Latch data into DAC
PortO = PortOut(REGC, 16)
'Display scroll bar setting
Text1.Text = Str$(inval)
'Display equivalent voltage setting
Text2.Text = Format$(Invalvolt, "##.##")
End Sub
```

Command button

On exiting from the program, Form 1 is unloaded and the program terminated.

```
Private Sub Command1_Click()
'Remove program and close
```

```
Unload Form1
End
End Sub
```

Declarations

The Form is completed by declaring a list of the variables used in the program and these are placed in the *General* section.

```
'Declare parameters
Const REGA = 0
Const REGB = REGA + 1
Const REGC = REGA + 2
Const CREG = REGA + 3
Private out%
Private Polarity As Integer
Private inval As Integer
Private Invalvolt As Double
```

The Form is saved as 8dac.frm.

Completing the program

The only part of the program left to complete is accessing the DLL required for the *PortO* statement. Here the modularity of Visual Basic is demonstrated as the project only has to add the file *io_usb.bas* which was introduced in Chapter 3. The project is saved as 8dac.vbp and the files should be as shown in Table 6.3.

Project	Project1 (8dac.vbp)
Form	Form1 (8dac.frm)
module	module1 (io_usb.bas)

Table 6.3 The 8dac.vbp project files

Running the program

8DAC board is connected to Port A of the USB 24 I/O module using the 20-way ribbon connector. The output of the DAC should be connected to a digital multimeter set on Volts as shown in Figure 6.4.

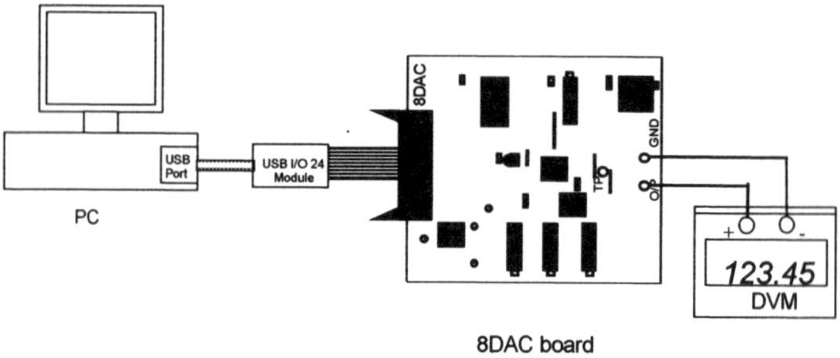

Figure 6.4 The 8DAC test circuit

An output is obtained from the DAC when the program is run. As the scroll bar setting is changed the voltage output will change. Check the polarity setting on the 8DAC board and also on the Form. Figure 6.5 illustrates the Form when the program is running.

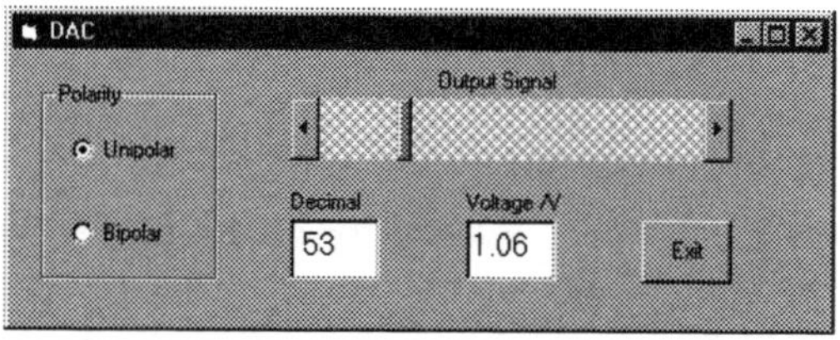

Figure 6.5 The 8DAC Form in operation

Exercise 6

6.1 Include in your program a method of enabling the voltage to be ramped up and down.

The scroll bar can be used to select the rate of the ramp and another scroll bar can be used to select the percentage of the ramp to be used.

Option buttons can be used to select rise or fall of the ramp.

6.2 Modify the original program to produce a sinusoidal output of varying rates and amplitudes.

Use a storage oscilloscope to display the outputs.

6.3 Repeat Exercise 6.2 for a square wave.

Summary

The DAC program is an extension of the programs used for the User Port Tester and the stepper motor. The exercises illustrate the possible range of applications the DACs possess. Their major limitations are the voltage ranges available and the speed of response of the output signal. The voltage range can be easily changed by suitable choice of output amplifiers. To improve the speed of response of the output signal will mean programming in C and creating a DLL to be called from the Visual Basic program. This is beyond the scope of this book but is certainly not a difficult task for an experienced C programmer.

7

8-bit ADC

8-bit Analogue to Digital Converter

There are several methods of converting analogue signals into digital form. These include flash encoders, integrating conversion, successive approximation conversion and sigma-delta conversion.

The flash encoder performs very fast conversions, and it is used in transient recorders and video cameras but tends to be very expensive. The design of the sigma-delta converter was proposed in the 1960s but it had to wait until the development of large-scale integration on silicon chips in the 1980s before it went into mass production. Its cost is now reasonable because of their extensive use in the domestic market and they are available as 16-, 20- and 24-bit versions.

In instrumentation the two most common Analogue to Digital Converters (ADCs) are the integrating and successive approximation converters. The integrating converter produces very accurate noisefree digital signals but tends to be relatively slow in performing the process.

A compromise in speed, accuracy and cost of all the currently available converters is the successive approximation analogue to digital converter. It is a good general purpose device which has a wide range of applications in the laboratory.

The 8ADC board considered in this chapter is based on an 8-bit successive approximation converter which can be used in either the unipolar or bipolar mode of operation

Unipolar and Bipolar

An ADC encodes an analogue signal into a digital number. Each digital number encompasses a range or quanta of analogue voltages. Like the DAC introduced in Chapter 6 the smallest quanta of input that the ADC can produce depends upon the LSB (Least Significant Bit). A factor which affects the size of the LSB is whether the analogue range is entirely positive or entirely negative (unipolar) or both negative and positive (bipolar).

In the case of an 8-bit ADC with a nominal Full Scale (FS) of 5.12V input the corresponding digital outputs are given in Table 7.1.

	Binary Output	Analogue Input
+FS - 1 LSB	1111 1111	+5.10V
1 LSB	0000 0001	+0.02V
0	0000 0000	0V

Table 7.1 Unipolar 8-bit ADC

FS - Full scale, i.e. Maximum positive or negative analogue input

LSB - Least Significant Bit, i.e. smallest incremental digital change

If the input range is bipolar and extends from –5.12V to +5.08V the digital outputs are shown in Table 7.2.

	Binary Output	Analogue Input
+FS - 1 LSB	1111 1111	+5.08V
1 LSB	1000 0001	+0.04V
0	1000 0000	0V
-1LSB	0111 1111	–0.04V
- FS	0000 0000	–5.12V

Table 7.2 Bipolar 8-bit ADC

If Tables 7.1 and 7.2 are compared it can be seen that the MSB is used as a sign bit for bipolar operation, i.e. 0 denotes negative, 1 is positive.

Theory of Operation

To actually program the ADCs it is also useful to understand the manner in which they operate.

The 8ADC board uses the ADC0804 ADC which is a successive approximation device. Figure 7.1 shows a block diagram of the essential features of such an ADC.

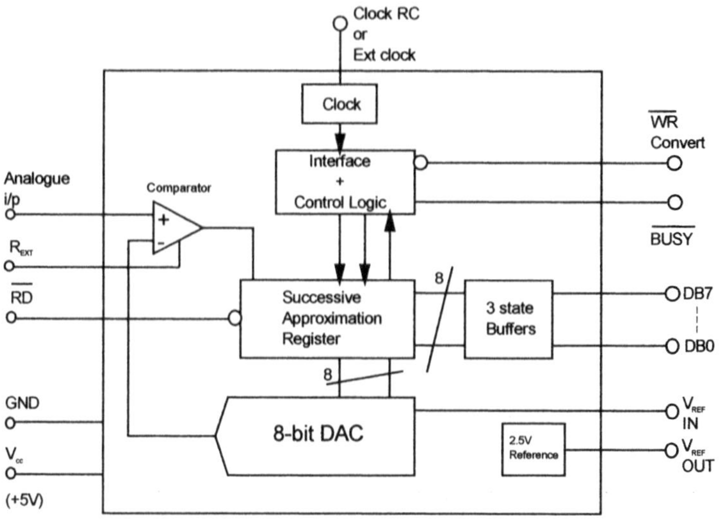

Figure 7.1 A successive approximation ADC

Basically the input voltage is compared to a reference voltage which is produced by the internal DAC. The successive approximation register generates a digital output at each clock pulse and controls the DAC output which will eventually equal the input voltage. The use of a comparator enables the digital output of the successive approximation register to either increase or decrease in response to the DAC output being either greater or smaller than the input voltage. Figure 7.2 shows the signals generated within the ADC at each clock pulse.

When a low level signal is applied to both the CS (Chip Select) and WR (Write) line of the ADC, the ADC is put into a hold state with the BUSY line low and the MSB of the ADC set to logic 1. A positive transition of either the CS or WR line at a falling edge of a clock pulse starts the successive approximation process. A decision is made whether or not the MSB remains at logic 1 or drops to logic 0 depending upon whether the input voltage is greater or smaller than the DAC output. At the next clock pulse the next bit is set and on the falling edge of a clock pulse this bit is left at logic 1 or changed to logic 0 depending again on the relative magnitude of the input signal with respect to the DAC output. The process continues and is completed when all 8 bits have made a decision and the BUSY line then goes high. The process takes a maximum of 8 clock cycles even though the input voltage and DAC output may have balanced earlier.

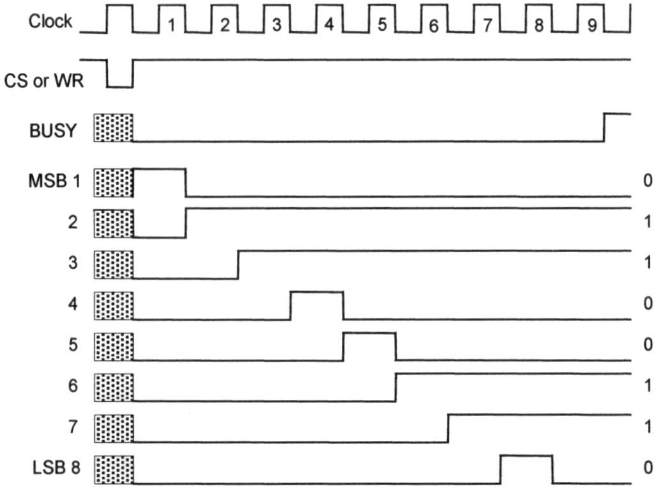

Figure 7.2 Successive approximation ADC waveforms

The 8ADC board

The 8ADC board is based upon an AD0804 8-bit successive approximation analogue to digital converter. This device is manufactured by several companies including National Semiconductors, Intersil and Philips. In the free running state it has a quoted conversion rate of 13690 conversions per second, and it may be used in either the unipolar (0V to +5V) or bipolar (–5V to +5V) input mode. The accuracy of the device is ±1LSB.

The ADC0804 has an internal clock, and conversions can be initiated by having both CS and WR inputs low and then allowing one to go high. On the 8ADC board the CS line is used to start conversions and the only other connections are +5V, 0V, and 8 data lines. These are all provided by the USB I/O 24 module. The end of conversion signal is not monitored.

Use of the 8ADC board

A slide switch on the 8ADC board (Figure 7.3) enables it to be used in either unipolar or bipolar mode.

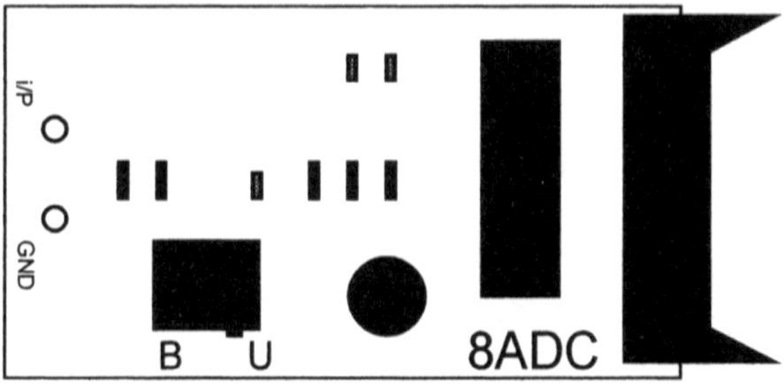

Figure 7.3 The 8ADC board

In position B (Bipolar position) input voltages in the range –5.12V to +5.08V can be used and the code used is offset binary. In position U (Unipolar position) input voltages in the range 0V to +5.10V can be used and these will be converted into a binary code. Full constructional details of the 8ADC board are supplied in the Appendix.

Input voltages are applied to the 8ADC using the two 4mm terminals and the board is connected to the USB I/O 24 module using the 20-way ribbon cable (Figure 7.4).

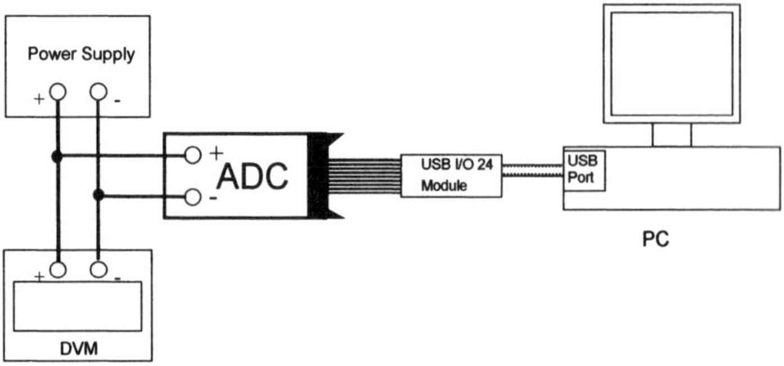

Figure 7.4 Connections for using an ADC with the PC

Program

Start up Visual Basic, select **New Project** and display Form1 on the screen.

In the *Properties* window for Form1 change Caption to *8ADC*.

Figure 7.5 shows the arrangement of Form1.

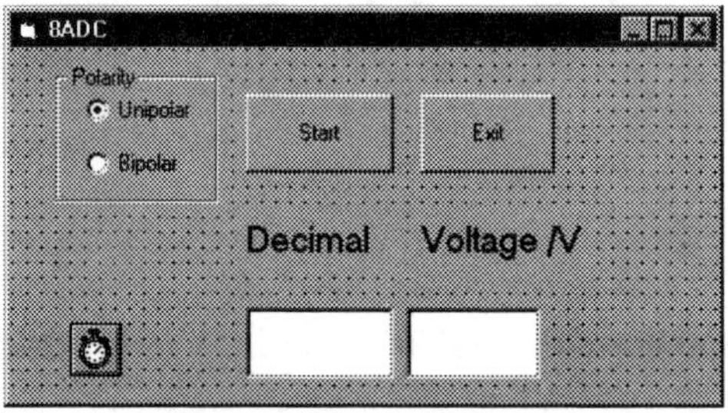

Figure 7.5 Layout of Form1

In the top left-hand corner place a Frame and change its Caption in the Properties window to *Polarity*.

Within this Frame place two Option Buttons, one above the other as shown.

Make the Captions for these two Buttons *Unipolar* and *Bipolar*. The Value property of the Unipolar Button is made *True*.

Alongside the Frame place two Command Buttons which have the Captions *Start* and *Exit*.

Below the Command Button place two Labels with Captions *Decimal* and *Voltage/V*.

Two Text Boxes are placed below the Labels. The Text in the Text Boxes should be cleared with the spacebar.

The last control to be placed on the Form is the Timer which should be placed at the bottom left-hand corner. The Interval and Enabled properties should be set to *500* and *False* respectively.

Inserting Code

Initially code should be attached to the Form and buttons.

The Form

This initiates the Unipolar option button.

```
Private Sub Form_Load()
'Initialise Polarity
Polarity = 0
End Sub
```

The Option Buttons

Each Option Button is assigned a state for Polarity which is used to determine the voltage equivalent of the decimal signal read by the USB I/O 24 module.

```
Private Sub Option1_Click()
'Set Polarity flag to Unipolar
Polarity = 0
End Sub
```

```
Private Sub Option2_Click()
'Set Polarity flag to Bipolar
Polarity = 1
End Sub
```

The Timer Control

This calls the Capture routine which initiates the 8ADC board and the Display routine which puts the Decimal and Voltage readings on to the screen.

```
Private Sub Timer1_Timer()
'Goto Capture
Capture
'Goto Display
Display
End Sub
```

The Command Buttons

The left-hand button is used to Start and Stop the reading of the ADC. This it does by enabling and disabling the Timer control. The caption of the button also changes.

```
Private Sub Command1_Click()
'Toggle Timer1
Timer1.Enabled = Not Timer1.Enabled
'Toggle Command1 caption
If Command1.Caption = "Start" Then
Command1.Caption = "Stop"
Else
```

```
Command1.Caption = "Start"
End If
End Sub
```

```
Private Sub Command2_Click()
'Remove program and close
Unload Form1
End
End Sub
```

Declarations

All of the parameters used in the program have to be declared and this is done under Declarations. This will include the addresses of the registers for Ports A, B and C and the control register.

```
'Declare parameters
Const REGA = 0
Const REGB = REGA + 1
Const REGC = REGA + 2
Const CREG = REGA + 3
Private out%
Private Polarity As Integer
Private inval As Integer
Private Invalvolt As Double
```

The Procedures

There are two procedures which appear in the general part of the program. These can be created by typing in *Private Sub Capture()* such that the procedure is then created or by using the **Tools/Add Procedure** menus.

Capture initiates the USB I/O 24 module. It has been written so that it can be adapted for use with either Port A or B.

Port A will be used.

The process for activitating the 8ADC is as follows:

1. Send start conversion pulse by making CS high (Control line 2 low to high).
2. After a delay, take CS low to permit data latch to be read (Control line 2 low).
3. Read data.

This is encoded in the following way:

```
Private Sub Capture()
'Switch off timer
Timer1.Enabled = False
'Configure USB I/O 24 module
out% = 147
PortO = PortOut(CREG, out%)
'Control line 2 high
PortO = PortOut(REGC, 16)
'Delay
For k = 1 To 1000: Next k
'Control line 2 low
PortO = PortOut(REGC, 0)
'Read ADC
inval = PortIn(REGA)
'Switch on timer
Timer1.Enabled = True
'Check for any keyboard interrupts
```

```
DoEvents
End Sub
```

Doevents ensures that the keyboard can be used to interrupt the program at any time.

The Display function checks the state of the Polarity flag and determines the voltage reading in either the Unipolar or Bipolar mode. It also places the ADC readings in the appropriate text boxes.

```
Private Sub Display()
'Select equivalent voltage settings
If Polarity = 0 Then
invalvolt = (5.10 * inval) / 255
Else
invalvolt = (inval - 128) * 5.12/ 128
End If
'Display ADC decimal reading
Text1.Text = Str$(inval)
'Display ADC voltage reading
Text2.Text = Format$(invalvolt, "##.##")
End Sub
```

The file should be saved as 8adc.frm. The file io_usb.bas should be added so that the Project window contains the following information (Table 7.3).

Project	Project1 (8adc.vbp)
Form	Form1 (8adc.frm)
module	module1 (io_usb.bas)

Table 7.3 The 8adc.vbp project files

The project should be saved as 8adc.vbp.

Equipment

The equipment required to use the 8ADC consists of an 8ADC board, laboratory power supply (0-30V, 2A) and a digital voltmeter (DVM).

The equipment is connected to the PC as shown in Figure 7.4.

The 8ADC board should be connected to the USB I/O 24 module by the 20-way ribbon cable.

Running the program

Set the switch on the 8ADC board to Unipolar and run the program. Switch on the power supply, vary the input voltage applied to the 8ADC board and observe the change in readings on the screen. Figure 7.6 shows some typical readings.

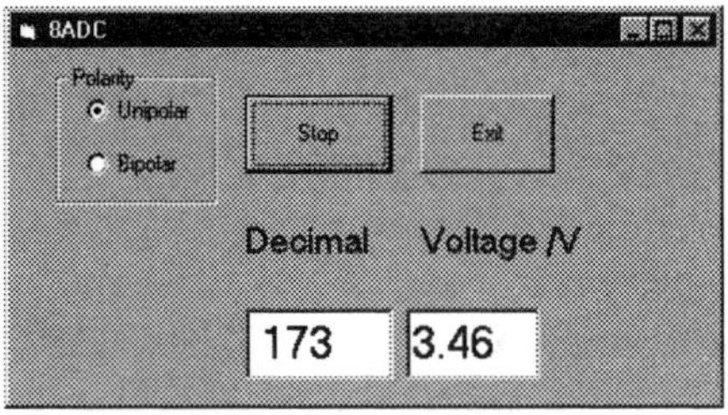

Figure 7.6 Readings from the 8ADC

Exercise 7

7.1 Test the program with the 8ADC switch set to both Unipolar and Bipolar modes.

You will have to reverse the connections from the power supply to obtain negative voltages.

7. 2 Modify the program so that it either stops when 500 readings have been taken or when any key is pressed on the keyboard.

7. 3 Use a CMDialog control to add Save, SaveAs and Print dialog boxes to the program.

7.4 Adapt the program so that the voltages are captured at 1 second intervals and displayed graphically.

7.5 Check the frequency range of the 8ADC by applying a sinusoidal signal to the 8ADC and observing the waveform on the screen.

What happens when the switch is set

a) in the unipolar position,

b) in the bipolar position?

7.6 A simple signal processing technique is to take a number of readings, e.g. 16, and average them before displaying them.

This can be achieved quite simply by modifying the Timer routine so that each time a reading is taken it is added to a running total. When 16 readings have been taken an average can be taken and displayed. The counter and the running total are then zeroed and the process recommenced.

The Timer routine will require the following modification:

```
Private Sub Timer1_Timer()
'Recover previous counter value
Static j
'Goto Capture
Capture
'Summate ADC readings
adcsum = adcsum + inval
'Increment adc reading counter
```

```
j = j + 1
'Check for 16 ADC readings
If j > 16 Then
'Average adc readings
inval = Int(adcsum / 16)
'Reset counter and ADC sum
j = 1
adcsum = 0
'Goto Display
Display
End If
End Sub
```

Static j ensures that the counter value from the previous pass through the routine is retained.

Modify the original 8adc.vbp program so that this signal averaging can be used and remember that Declarations and Load will require some changes.

7. 7 Connect a thermistor and a 1k resistor in series to a power supply. Maintain a constant voltage of 5V across the two components and monitor the p.d. developed across the thermistor using a DVM. Crocodile clips are ideal for making the connections.

Heat the thermistor, e.g by bringing it close to a lamp bulb and observe the change in voltage on the DVM.

7. 8 When the system is working correctly, replace the DVM with the 8ADC and plot a cooling curve of the thermistor.

Summary

The 8ADC board has many general-purpose applications and will find numerous applications in project work. Its major disadvantage is that it is sensitive to noise but this can be turned to its advantage if it is used to experiment with different signal processing techniques.

The Visual Basic programs do not reveal the full capabilities of the 8ADC. If the reader has experience of C programming it may be advantageous to translate the Capture sub-routine into C, compile as a DLL and then incorporate the resulting DLL into the Visual Basic display Form. This procedure is beyond the scope of this book but it can provide an excellent program for reasonably fast data acquisition.

12-bit ADC

12-bit Analogue to Digital Conversion

The 8-bit successive approximation ADC is very good for performing reasonably fast analogue to digital conversion but it is very susceptible to noise and spurious signals. Integrating ADCs are slower but their design ensures that noise is reduced significantly. The 12ADC board is based upon a dual-ramp integrating ADC, which uses the same timing system to measure an unknown voltage which is then compared with a reference voltage. This makes the 12ADC board ideal for use with thermocouples and strain gauges in bridge circuits where accuracy of the reading is far more important than speed of data acquisition.

12ADC resolution

The dual-ramp integrating ADC chip used in the 12ADC board has a quite different mode of presenting its digital data compared to that of the 8ADC board. The 12ADC board data output has a sign bit as well as the data bits.

In the case of a 12-bit ADC this means that there are 4095 quanta in the positive sense and 4095 quanta in the negative sense. The device is bipolar and may be regarded as having a 12-bit resolution in both senses. If the ADC has an LSB equivalent voltage of +1mV, the inputs for such an ADC can range from –4.095V to +4.095V. The corresponding binary outputs are given in Table 8.1.

	Sign bit	Binary Output	Analogue Input
+FS	1	1111 1111 1111	+4.095V
+1 LSB	1	0000 0000 0001	+0.001V
0	1	0000 0000 0000	+0.000V
-1 LSB	0	0000 0000 0001	–0.001V
-FS	0	1111 1111 1111	–4.095V

Table 8.1 12-bit ADC with sign bit

Theory of Operation of the dual-ramp integrating ADC

The 12ADC board is built around the ICL7109CPL which is a dual-ramp integrating ADC. The principle of operation of a dual-ramp ADC is dependent upon a capacitor which is charged up by the input voltage and discharged under the control of a reference voltage. The relative times of charge and discharge determine the amount by which the counter is incremented by a number of clock pulses. Figure 8.1 shows a schematic of the circuit.

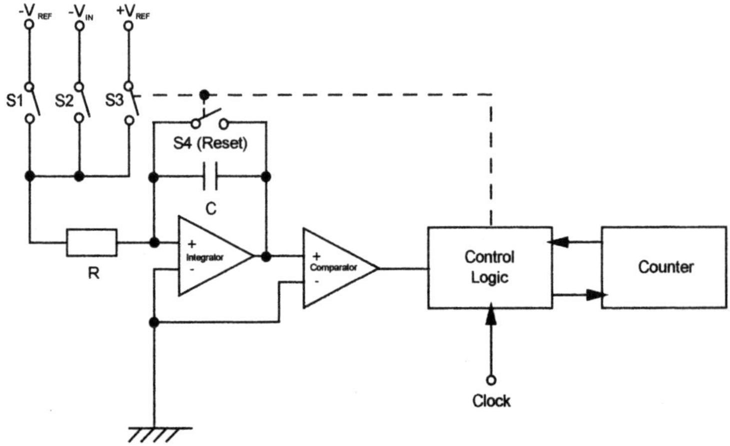

Figure 8.1 A dual-ramp integrating ADC

Initially the input voltage is connected to the integrator in which the capacitor C is charged up. This causes the comparator to keep the gate open enabling clock pulses to be applied to the counter. The counter increments until it is fully loaded. It then clocks over into the unloaded state and transmits a pulse to the switch control. This disconnects the input voltage and connects the reference voltage to the integrator. The reference voltage is negative and causes the capacitor C to discharge. The gate remains open while the capacitor is discharged until the integrator output is zero and about to become negative. The gate is closed and no more pulses reach the counter. The number stored in the counter is proportional to the input voltage.

This may be proved as follows:

Figure 8.2 shows the voltage output of the integrator as the capacitor charges and discharges. The slopes are linear since the time constant RC is relatively large.

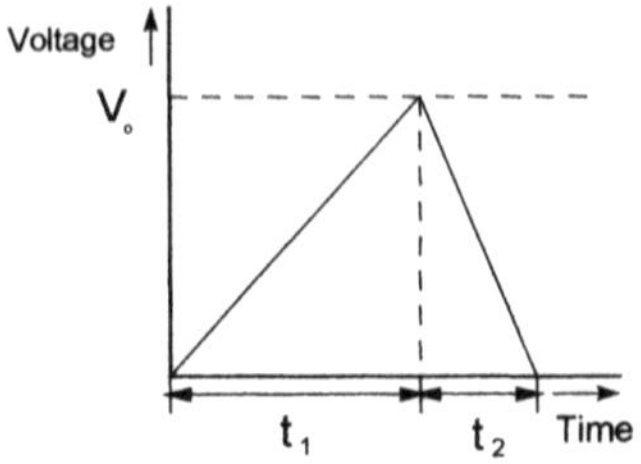

Figure 8.2 Voltage output of the integrator

If the time taken for the capacitor to charge up under control of the integrator is t_1, the capacitor voltage is $V_o(t_1)$. V_i is the input voltage.

$$V_0(t_1) = \int_0^{t_1} \frac{1}{CR} V_i dt = \frac{V_i t_1}{CR}$$

The capacitor now discharges from $V_o(t_1)$ in the time t_2. The integrator output voltage $V_o(t_2)$ is given by:

$$V_0(t_2) = \frac{V_{ref} t_2}{CR}$$

where V_{ref} is the reference voltage.

Since $V_o(t_1) = V_o(t_2)$ - (see Figure 8.2),

$$\frac{V_i t_1}{CR} = \frac{V_{ref} t_2}{CR}$$

and $V_i t_1 = V_{ref} t_2$.

Hence $$V_i = \frac{V_{ref} t_2}{t_1}$$

If the clock is producing pulses at a regular rate of n per second

$N_1 = nt_1$ and $N_2 = nt_2$.

Therefore $$V_i = \frac{V_{ref} N_2}{N_1}$$

V_{ref} / N_1 may be replaced by a constant K since V_{ref} is a constant and N_1 is the value of the loaded counter.

Therefore $V_i = KN_2$.

i.e. $V_i \propto N_2$

If the input signal is negative, the capacitor will charge up in the negative direction. This will be sensed by the control logic which will switch in a positive reference voltage causing the capacitor to charge up in the positive direction. The graph in Figure 8.2 will be inverted. The net result will be same, with the unknown voltage V_i being proportional to the counter reading, N_2 but with the sign bit set for negative.

The main disadvantage of the dual-ramp integrating ADC is that it is relatively slow acquiring this charge and then discharging the capacitor. The major advantage is that it integrates the input signal and removes any spurious noise signals that may occur.

Dual-Ramp Integrating Analogue to Digital Conversion

There are many occasions in the laboratory when it is necessary to measure small voltages, e.g. microvolts. A dual-ramp integrating analogue to digital converter is ideal for such purposes since it can produce results with a high degree of reproducibility and accuracy. The major disadvantage of such ADCs is that they tend to be slow, i.e. conversion times in the order of tens of milliseconds but this is not too problematic in the laboratory environment where many sensors and transducers require long (in computer speed terms) times to acquire their readings.

The12ADC board is a 12-bit analogue to digital converter which can be used in the range of ±4.095V. It may be used with the USB I/O 24 module fitted to a PC. The board is based upon an ICL7109CPL device which has an auto zero facility and outputs its digital data in a high and low byte format. The high byte contains bits signifying polarity, overrange and the 4 most significant bits of digital data and the low byte has the 8 remaining bits of data. Figure 8.3 shows the appearance of the 12ADC board.

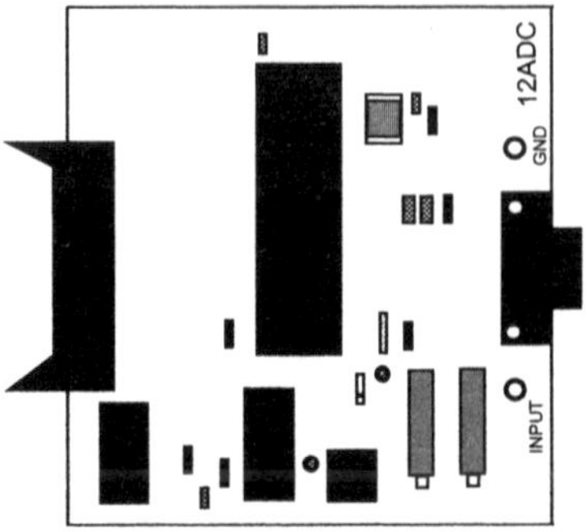

Figure 8.3 12ADC board layout

In order to make measurements at lower voltages it is necessary to insert a pre-amplifier between the signal source, i.e. the sensor or transducer, and the 12ADC board. The Variable Gain Programmable Amplifier (VGPA) board serves this particular purpose (Figure 8.4).

The VGPA board uses an AD524 precision instrumentation amplifier and increases the sensitivity of the 12-bit ADC board. The VGPA board contains a pre-amplifier input stage which has a gain that can be set to x1, x10, x100 and x1000. This gives the following voltage ranges:

x1	–4.095V	to	+4.095V
x10	–409.5mV	to	+409.5mV
x100	–40.95mV	to	+40.95mV
x1000	–4.095mV	to	+4.095mV

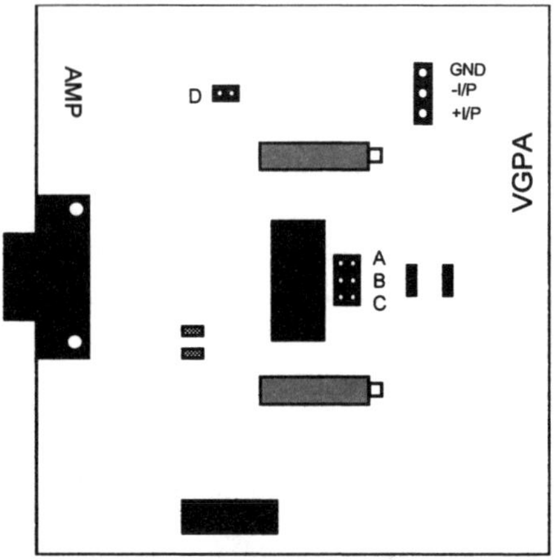

Figure 8.4 The VGPA board

Method of obtaining the data

A feature of the 12ADC board is that it has an 8-bit digital output yet it is capable of producing a resolution of 12 bits accompanied by a sign and overrange bit. This is achieved by introducing some additional circuitry on the board which enables the lowest 8 bits, i.e. the low byte, to be read separately from the highest 8 bits, i.e. the high byte. (2 of these bits are subsequently discarded).

Figure 8.5 shows a schematic of the input circuitry that is used to access the high and low data bytes. This consists of a D-type flip-flop which is toggled by a control signal pulse.

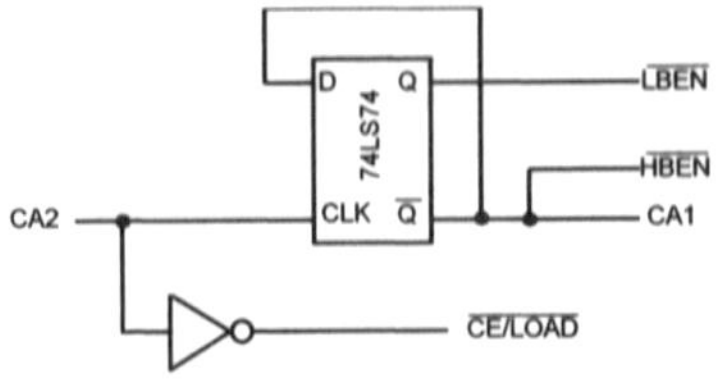

Figure 8.5 Circuit used to access high and low bytes

The data is accessed by the PC by transmitting a control signal on Control line 2 (CA2 or CB2) of the interface board to read the high byte followed by another control signal on Control line 2 to read the low byte. The problem that arises is that the system has to be initialised so that the bytes are read in the correct order. This check is performed by using Control line 1 (CA1 or CB1) to indicate when the high byte is ready to be read. The sequence of events using Port A is indicated in Figure 8.6.

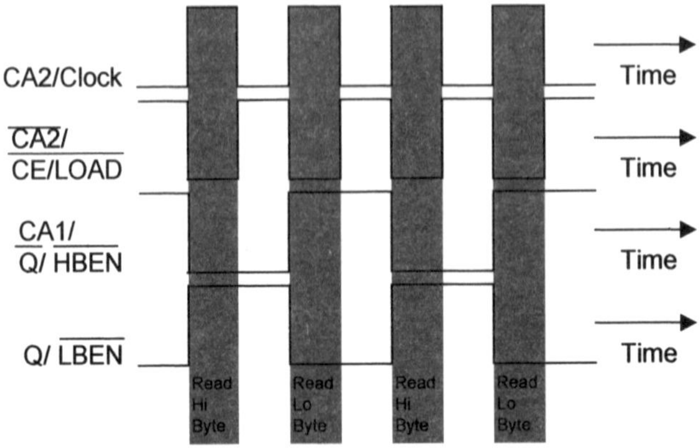

Figure 8.6 Sequence to obtain high and low bytes

Program

Start up Visual Basic, select **New Project** and display Form1 on the screen.

In the Properties window for Form1 change Caption to *12ADC*.

Figure 8.7 shows the arrangement of Form1.

In the top left-hand corner place a Frame and change its Caption in the Properties window to *Gain.*

Within this Frame place four Option Buttons one above the other as shown.

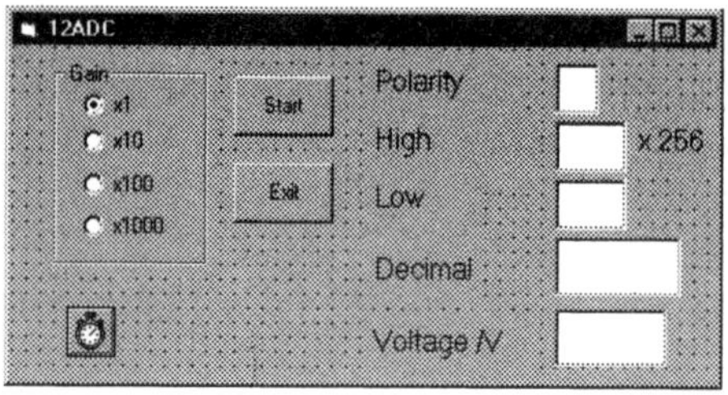

Figure 8.7 Layout of Form1

Make the Captions for these four Buttons *x1, x10, x100* and *x1000.* The Value property of the x1 is made *True.*

Place alongside the Frame two Command Buttons which have the Captions *Start* and *Exit* as shown in Figure 8.7.

Place five Labels with Captions *Polarity*, *High*, *Low*, *Decimal* and *Voltage/V* on to the Form.

Five Text Boxes are placed alongside the Labels. The Text in the Text Boxes should be cleared with the spacebar.

A further Label is placed adjacent to the second Text Box down (see Figure 8.7) and its Caption should be changed to x256.

The last control to be placed on the Form is the Timer which should be placed at the bottom left-hand corner. The Interval and Enabled properties should be set to *500* and *False* respectively

Inserting Code

Initially code should be attached to the Form and buttons.

The Form

This initiates the Gain option button and ensures that the displayed voltages are set for unity gain.

```
Private Sub Form_Load()
'Initialise Gain variable
Gain = 1000
End Sub
```

The Option Buttons

Each Option Button is assigned a state for the Gain which is used to determine the voltage equivalent of the decimal signal read by the USB I/O 24 module. With each Gain there is a setting for the label associated with the Voltage display.

```
Private Sub Option1_Click()
'Set Gain
Label5.Caption = "Voltage /V"
Gain = 1000
End Sub
```

```
Private Sub Option2_Click()
'Set Gain
Label5.Caption = "Voltage /mV"
Gain = 10
End Sub
```

```
Private Sub Option3_Click()
'Set Gain
Label5.Caption = "Voltage /mV"
Gain = 100
```

```
End Sub
```

```
Private Sub Option4_Click()
'Set Gain
Label5.Caption = "Voltage /mV"
Gain = 1000
End Sub
```

The Timer Control

This calls the Capture routine which initiates the 12ADC board and the Display routine which puts the Decimal and Voltage readings on to the screen.

```
Private Sub Timer1_Timer()
'Goto Capture
Capture
'Goto Display
Display
End Sub
```

The Command Buttons

The left-hand button is used to Start and Stop the reading of the ADC. This it does by enabling and disabling the Timer control. The Caption of the button also changes.

```
Private Sub Command1_Click()
'Toggle Timer1
Timer1.Enabled = Not Timer1.Enabled
'Toggle Command1 caption
If Command1.Caption = "Start" Then
```

```
Command1.Caption = "Stop"
Else
Command1.Caption = "Start"
End If
End Sub
```

The right-hand button, i.e. the Exit button, unloads the Form prior to closing down the system.

```
Private Sub Command2_Click()
'Remove program and close
Unload Form1
End
End Sub
```

Declarations

All of the parameters used in the program have to be declared and this is done under Declarations.

```
'Declare parameters
Const REGA = 0
Const REGB = REGA + 1
Const REGC = REGA + 2
Const CREG = REGA + 3
Private out%
Private Gain As Single
Private HiX As Integer
Private LoX As Integer
Private inval As Integer
```

```
Private Invalvolt As Double
```

The Procedures

There are two procedures which appear in the general part of the program. These can be created by typing in *Private Sub Capture()* when the procedure is then created or by using the **Tools/Add Procedure** menus

Capture puts into practice the sequence of events that are shown in Figure 8.6. These are:

1. Transmit pulse(s) on Control line 2 until Control line 1 goes high.
2. Transmit pulse on Control line 2 and read high (Hi) byte.
3. Transmit pulse on Control line 2 and read low (Lo) byte.
4. Print (Hi byte * 256) + (Lo byte).
5. Repeat from 1.

The routine first configures the USB I/O 24 module, it then ensures that the 12ADC is set up to output the high and low bytes in the correct order and then it reads the ADC. The routine has been written so that it can be adapted for use with either Port A or B.

Port A will be used.

```
Private Sub Capture()
'Initialise High and Low bytes array
Static X(2) As Integer
'Configure USB I/O 24 module
out% = 147
PortO = PortOut(CREG, out%)
'Initialise 12ADC board
Do
'Control line 2 low
PortO = PortOut(REGC, 0)
```

```
'Control line 2 high
PortO = PortOut(REGC, 16)
'Control line 2 low
PortO = PortOut(REGC, 0)
'Check for control line 1
z% = PortIn(REGC) And 1
Loop While z% = 0
For I = 1 To 2
'Control line 2 high
PortO = PortOut(REGC, 16)
'Read ADC
X(I) = PortIn(REGA)
'Control line 2 low
PortO = PortOut(REGC, 0)
Next I
'Load High byte
HiX = X(1)
'Load Low byte
LoX = X(2)
End Sub
```

The *Display* function has the task of stripping the overrange and sign bit from the high byte, and it also checks the state of the Gain flag and determines the voltage reading. It places Polarity, the values of the high and low bytes and both of the ADC readings in the appropriate text boxes.

```
Private Sub Display()
'Determine polarity
```

```
Polarity = (HiX And &H20) / 32
Inval = (2 * Polarity - 1) * ((HiX And &HF) * 256 + LoX)
If Polarity = 1 Then
Text1.Text = "+"
Else
Text1.Text = "-"
End If
'Display High byte
Text2.Text = (HiX And &HF)
'Display Low byte
Text3.Text = LoX
'Adjust voltage for Gain setting
Invalvolt = Inval / Gain
'Display ADC decimal reading
Text4.Text = Str$(Inval)
'Display ADC voltage reading
Text5.Text = Format$(Invalvolt, "##.####")
End Sub
```

The file is saved as 12adc.frm and the file io_usb.bas should be added. The project is saved as 12adc.vbp and the files should be as shown in Table 8.2.

Project	Project1 (12adc.vbp)
Form	Form1 (12adc.frm)
module	module1 (io_usb.bas)

Table 8.2 The 12adc.vbp project files

Equipment

The equipment required to use the 12ADC consists of the 12ADC board, a laboratory power supply (0-30V, 2A) and a digital voltmeter (DVM). To monitor low voltages the VGPA board and a selection of resistors will also be required.

Running the program

Initially the 12ADC board should be connected to the USB I/O 24 module by the 20-way ribbon cable. A laboratory power supply should then be connected to the input of the 12ADC board.

The circuit layout is shown in Figure 8.8.

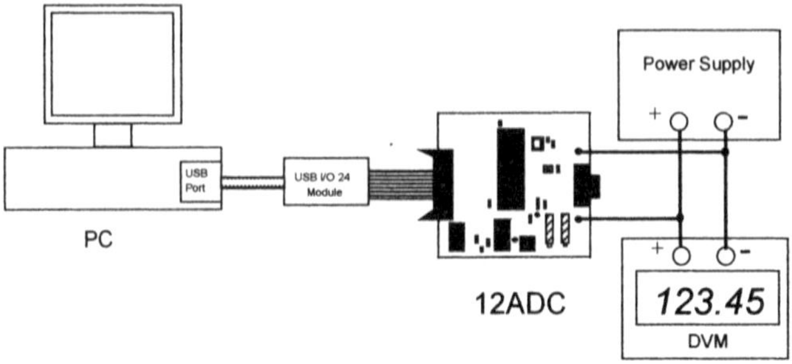

Figure 8.8 The 12ADC circuit layout

Set the gain on the 12ADC Form to Gain x1 and run the program. Switch on the power supply, vary the input voltage applied to the 12ADC board and observe the change in readings on the screen. Figure 8.9 shows the 12ADC Form when the program is running

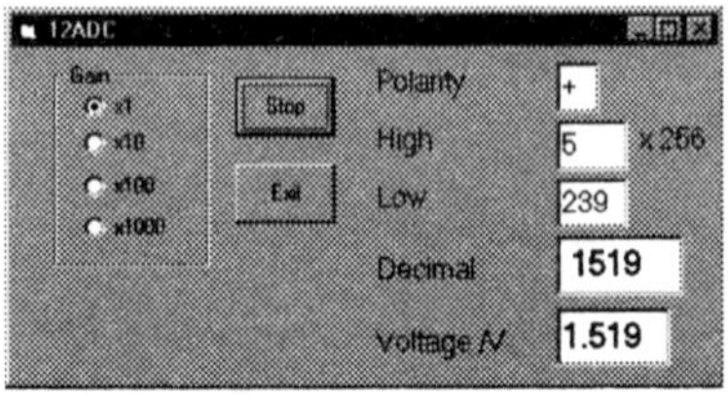

Figure 8.9 Display 12ADC data

Exercise 8.1

8.1.1 Set up the 12ADC board and use the program to check that it is operating correctly.

Apply both negative and positive voltage inputs to the board and investigate if there are any discrepancies in the readings that are obtained.

Monitor the input voltage with a DVM and compare the 12ADC readings.

8.1.2 Add option boxes and modify the program so that the 12ADC may be used on either Port A or Port B.

8.1.3 The stability of the 12ADC board may be verified by setting the input voltage to a particular value and checking the displayed reading over a period of time, e.g. 1 hour, 2 hour,.....24 hours!

8.1.4 Connect the 12 ADC to either an experiment or instrument which produces a voltage output in the range 0.000 to 4.095V and investigate whether the 12ADC can be used as a substitute for the normally used voltmeter.

8.1.5 Store your readings in an array and plot a graph in real time.

8.1.6 Use a CMDialog control to add Save, SaveAs and Print dialog boxes to the program.

Small signal measurement - Using the VGPA board

The programs used with the combined 12ADC and VGPA boards are identical to those used with the 12ADC board, with slight modifications in the Full Scale Range (FSR) to account for the voltage range that is being used. Figure 8.10 shows the circuit connections.

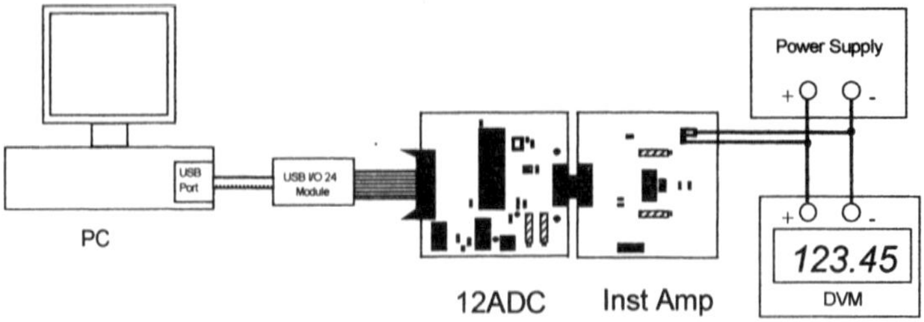

Figure 8.10 The 12ADC and VGPA circuit layout

Making connections to the VGPA board

There are 3 inputs to the VGPA board, a positive signal input, a negative signal input and a ground line (Figure 8.11).

In most circumstances it is necessary to connect the GND and -I/P together. The signal input should then be connected between the -I/P and +I/P lines. The board is connected to the 12ADC board using the 15 -pin D type connector.

Figure 8.11 Connections to the input of the VGPA board

Selecting the gain

The gain of the VGPA board is selected by jumpers A, B and C on the board. These are situated close to the input terminals and require the jumper connections to be made according to Figure 8.12.

Gain	Connection
X1	None
X10	A
X100	B
X1000	C

Figure 8.12 Selecting the gain of the VGPA board

Exercise 8.2

8.2.1 The program already written for the 12ADC can be used with the VGPA.

If the FSR of 4.095 mV, i.e. gain of 1000, is used it will be necessary to use the circuit in Figure 8.13 to attenuate the input of the power supply if this is used for test purposes.

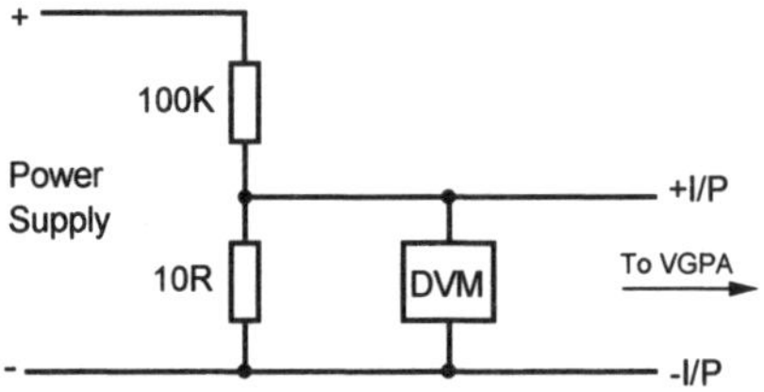

Figure 8.13 Potential divider circuit to reduce power supply output

Summary

The 12ADC board has many applications in instrumentation. Its good stability means that it can be used for temperature measurements as well as the host of applications involving strain gauges. What must always be remembered is that time has to be given for the conversion to take place. The time taken by the hardware to perform is compensated by the considerable reduction in signal processing required within the PC needed for other types of converting devices.

It is important to select the appropriate ADC for the task and in lots of respects this is the additional skill that has to be developed along with the skill of actually programming the device.

Appendix

The Interface Boards

This Appendix provides information about the circuit boards used in Chapters 4, 5, 6, 7 and 8. The circuit board designs have been developed in Aries 5.2 Professional produced by Labcenter Electronics.

Each board has two copper masks and a silk screen overlay showing the position of the components. One copper mask shows the component side view, the other is the track side view. A problem with any printing process is that it is very difficult to reproduce the masks in this Appendix to the dimensional accuracy required to fabricate the boards directly from the mask. With the exception of the 8ADC board which is 5cm x 10cm in size, all boards should be 10cm square.

To achieve these dimensions the relevant mask should be scanned and inserted into Microsoft Word for Windows. The resulting images can then be adjusted until the appropriate horizontal and vertical scales are achieved. Each copper PCB mask has scales attached.

The component side mask can be copied on to good quality tracing paper using a laser printer. Alternatively the track side mask can be used as a pattern with acetate sheet and crepe tape to produce the component layout.

The circuit board can then be produced by the normal procedure for manufacture of PCBs.

Accompanying each PCB mask and silk screen overlay in this Appendix is a list of components and details of the circuit. Included in the list of components is the name of a supplier and its catalogue number. The addresses of these suppliers are given in section A7.

Once a circuit is produced it can be tested with the program listed in the appropriate Chapter.

A1 The User Port Tester

The User Port Tester board is used to test the digital input/output signals passing through the USB I/O 24 module card. The board can provide the input 8-bit digital signals by throwing the appropriate switches of the DIL switch on the board. The 8-bit code generated is displayed on the LED bar code. The board can also display, on the same LED display, 8-bit binary codes being fed out of the PC. The two remaining bars indicate the status of the two control lines of the port being tested. The board will automatically operate in the correct mode, input/output, as set by the USB I/O 24 module.

A1.1 Circuit

Figure A1.1 shows one of the ten circuits that drive each of the LEDs. In the input mode the position of the switch determines whether a logic one or zero is applied to the data and control lines of the USB I/O 24 module. In the output mode the switch may be left in either position since the state of the LED is set by the USB I/O 24 module.

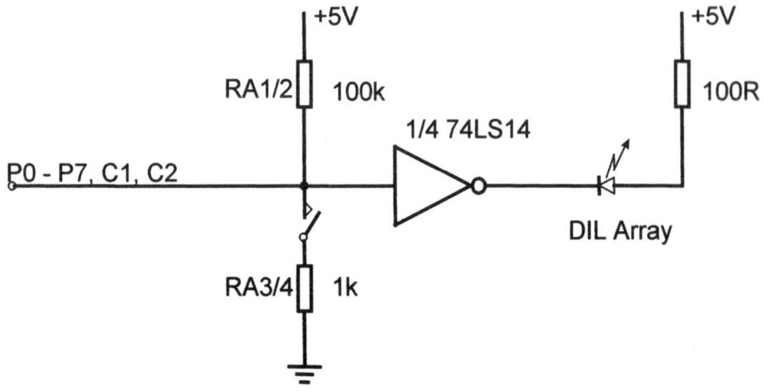

Figure A1.1 One LED driver circuit

A1.2 The Printed Circuit Boards

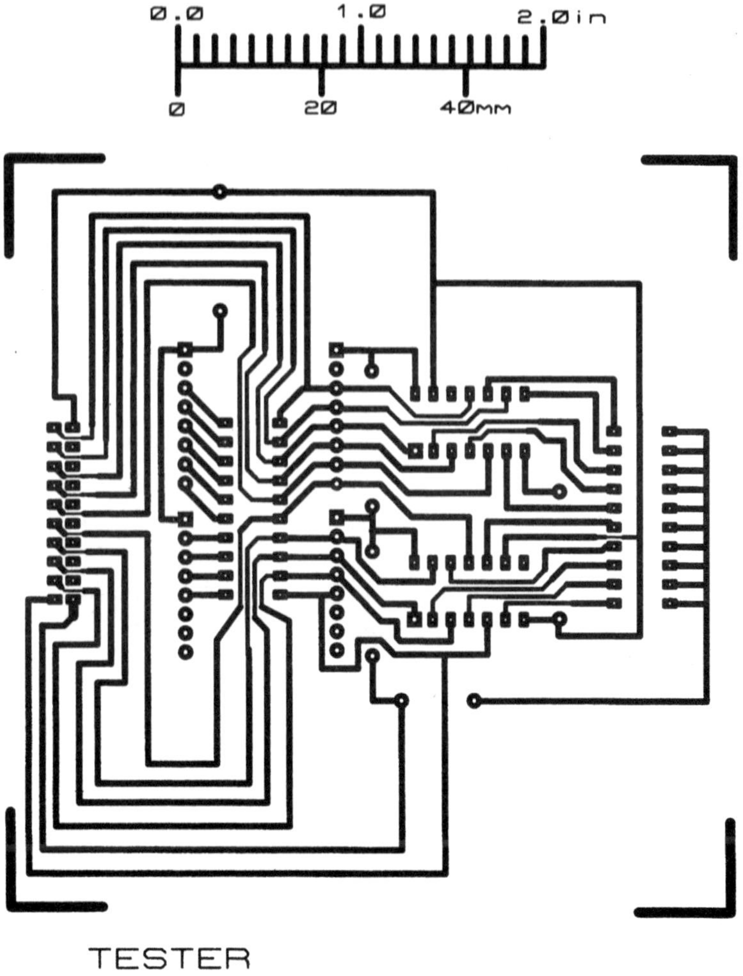

Figure A1.2 The User Port Tester PCB (Component side view)

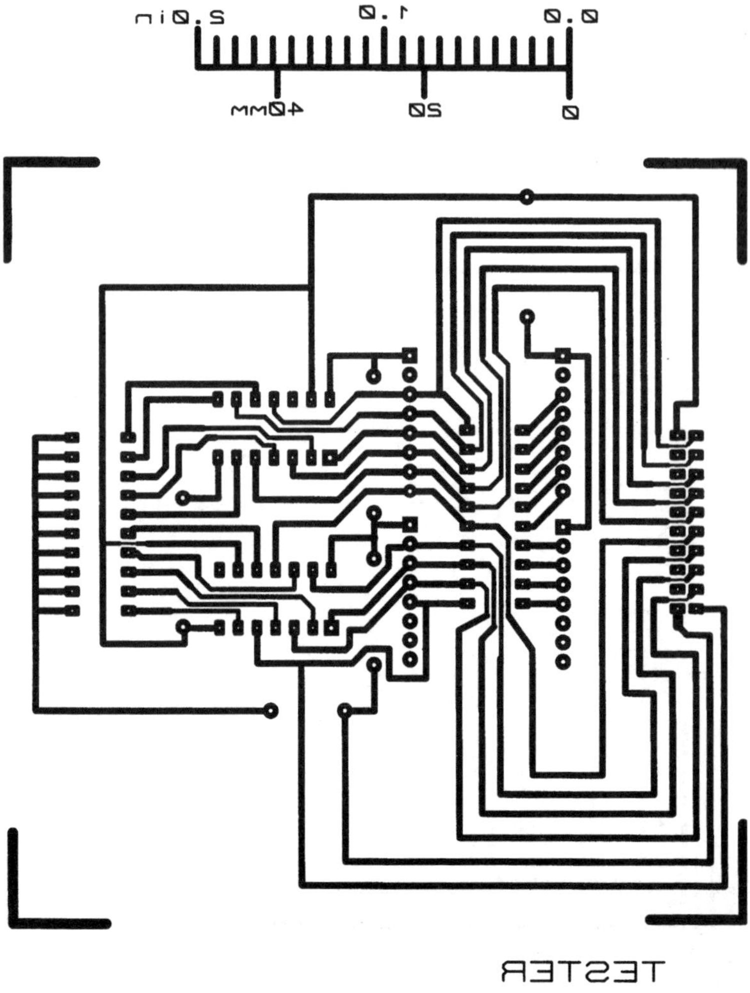

Figure A1.3 The User Port Tester PCB (Track side view)

1.3 Components

Figure A1.3 shows the layout of the components on the board.

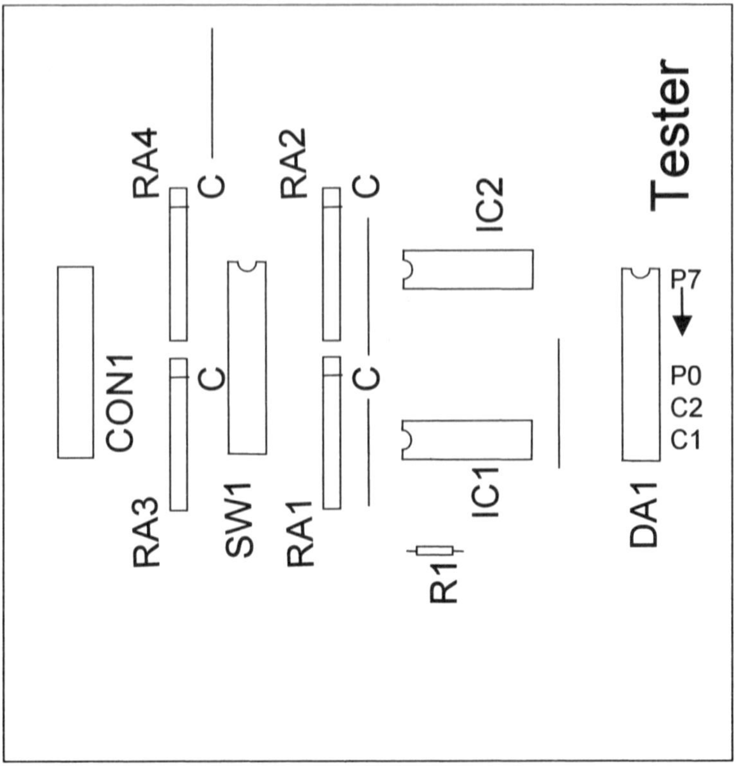

Figure A1.4 The User Port Tester board component layout

Resistors

RA1	100k	7 commoned	RS 168-718
RA2	100k	7 commoned	RS 168-718
RA3	1k	7 commoned	RS 168-516
RA4	1k	7 commoned	RS 168-516
R1	100R	0.4W tolerance ±5%	Farnell 332-574

Integrated Circuits

IC1	74LS14	Hex Schmitt inverters	Farnell 373-643
IC2	74LS14	Hex Schmitt inverters	Farnell 373-643

Switch

SW1	10-way	PCB SPST	Farnell 422-678

Connector

CON1	IDC	20-way connector	RS 471-137

LEDs

DA1	10	LED bar	Farnell 152-279

A2 The Stepper Motor board

Stepper motors are used in many applications requiring accurate positioning such as automatic machinery and robotics and in applications where continuous motion at variable speeds is controlled by a computer. They are available with a range of power and torque ratings to suit a wide range of applications.

A2.1 The Circuit

On the Stepper Motor board, a ULN 2064B Darlington driver chip is used to directly drive the coils. The pin configuration and the circuit for an individual stage is shown in Figure A2.1. The maximum supply voltage to the chip is 50V and the maximum current per stage is 1.5A. This supply can be connected to the board via terminal blocks.

The stepper motor is connected to the board via either terminal blocks or plug connectors.

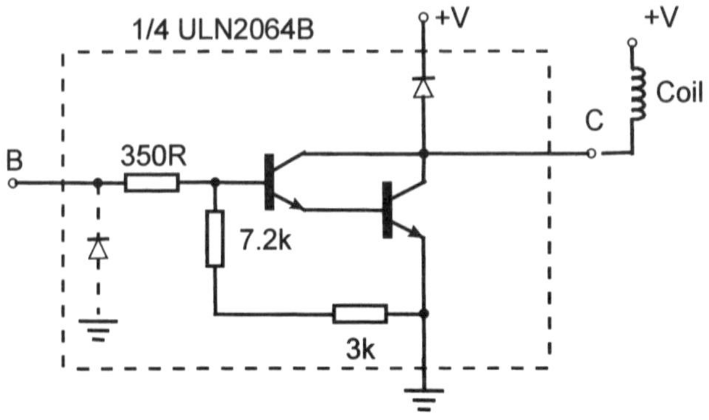

Figure A2.1 Circuit configuration for an individual stage

A2.2 The Printed Circuit Boards

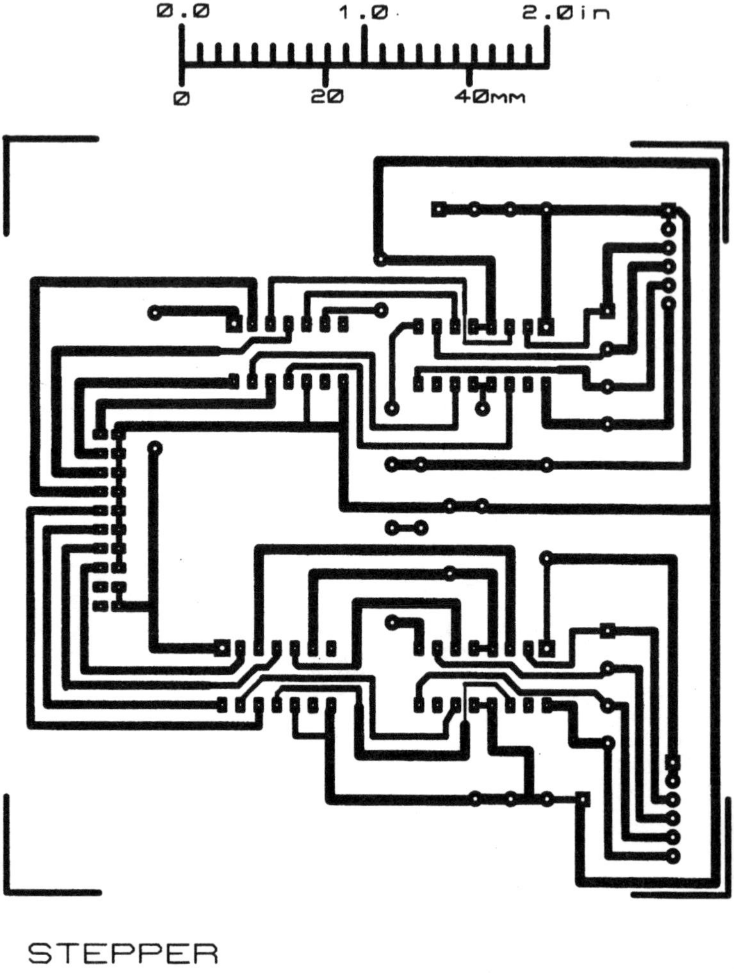

Figure A2.2 The Stepper Motor board PCB (Component side view)

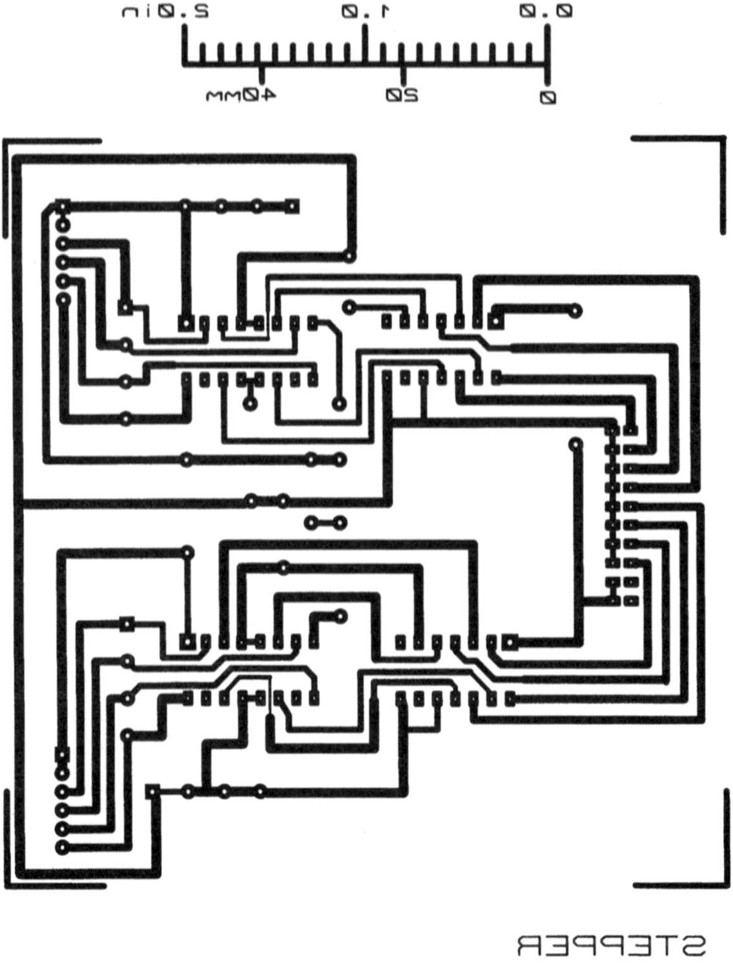

Figure A2.3 The Stepper Motor board PCB (Track side view)

A2.3 Components

Figure A2.4 shows the layout of the components on the board overlay.

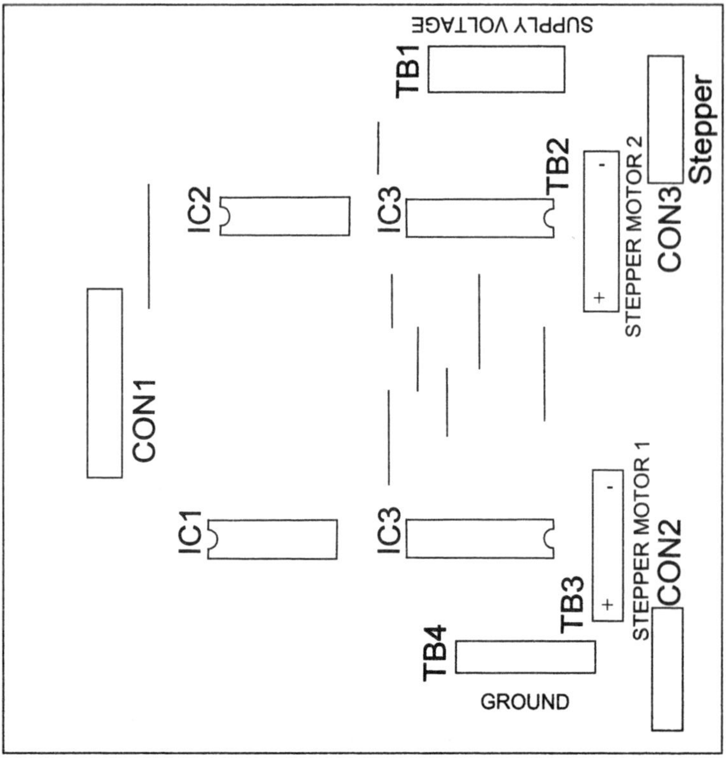

Figure A2.4 The Stepper Motor board component layout

Connectors

CON1		IDC 20-way connector	Farnell 152-279
CON2	6-way	PCB headers (snap to length)	Farnell 143-136
CON3	6-way	PCB headers (snap to length)	Farnell 143-136
TB1	4-way	PCB std mtd screw terminals	Farnell 344-4555
TB2	4-way	PCB std mtd screw terminals	Farnell 344-4555
TB3	4-way	PCB std mtd screw terminals	Farnell 344-4555
TB4	4-way	PCB std mtd screw terminals	Farnell 344-4555

Integrated Circuits

IC1	74LS04	Hex inverter	Farnell 373-450
IC2	74LS04	Hex Inverter	Farnell 373-450
IC3	ULN2064B	Quad Darlington driver	Farnell 409-790
IC4	ULN2064B	Quad Darlington driver	Farnell 409-790

A3 The 8DAC board

A digital to analogue converter is a device which produces an analogue output, i.e. a current or voltage, when a digital input is applied to it. The 8DAC board is a voltage output 8-bit digital to analogue converter (DAC) board based upon the Texas Instruments TLC7524 8-bit multiplying digital to analogue converter. The TLC7542 is interchangeable with Analog Devices AD7524, PMI PM-7524 and Micro Power Systems MP7524.

The 8DAC board can be used in either the unipolar (positive only output) or bipolar mode (positive and negative output) with a resolution of 255 steps between the maximum and minimum voltage outputs. The board is powered from the internal power supply of the PC. It is possible to obtain a full-scale range (FSR) of the voltage output up to a maximum of +5.12V in the unipolar mode. The selection of the DAC resolution is made using the on-board switch and the DAC is calibrated using a calibration routine and potentiometers. In bipolar mode the range extends from –2.56V up to +2.54V though this may be altered by adjustment of the appropriate potentiometers.

The USB I/O 24 module provides two ports to which the DAC board may be connected. Each port consists of 8 data lines which can be set up as either inputs or outputs, plus two control lines which are used as interrupt or pulse lines. These ports must be configured so that digital data can be transmitted to the 8DAC board. The digital data is latched into the DAC so that the analogue output will remain constant even when the DAC is not being addressed by the PC.

A3.1 The circuit

Figure A3.1 shows the TLC7524 (IC1) used in the 8DAC board. IC5 supplies the positive and negative voltage supplies to the two amplifiers

IC3 and IC4. IC3 provides the gain for the voltage output of IC1 and in the unipolar mode IC4 acts as an approximately times two gain amplifier. In the bipolar mode IC4 is used as a summing amplifier so that the board can produce both negative and positive voltage outputs. IC2 provides a 2.5V reference voltage for the circuit.

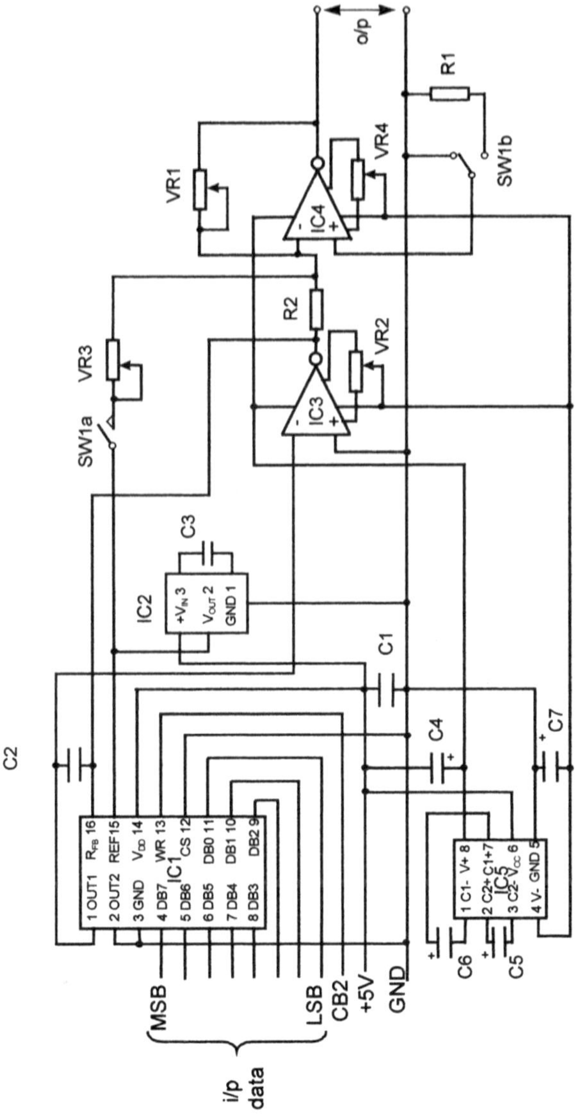

Figure A3.1 The 8DAC board circuit

A3.2 The Printed Circuit Boards

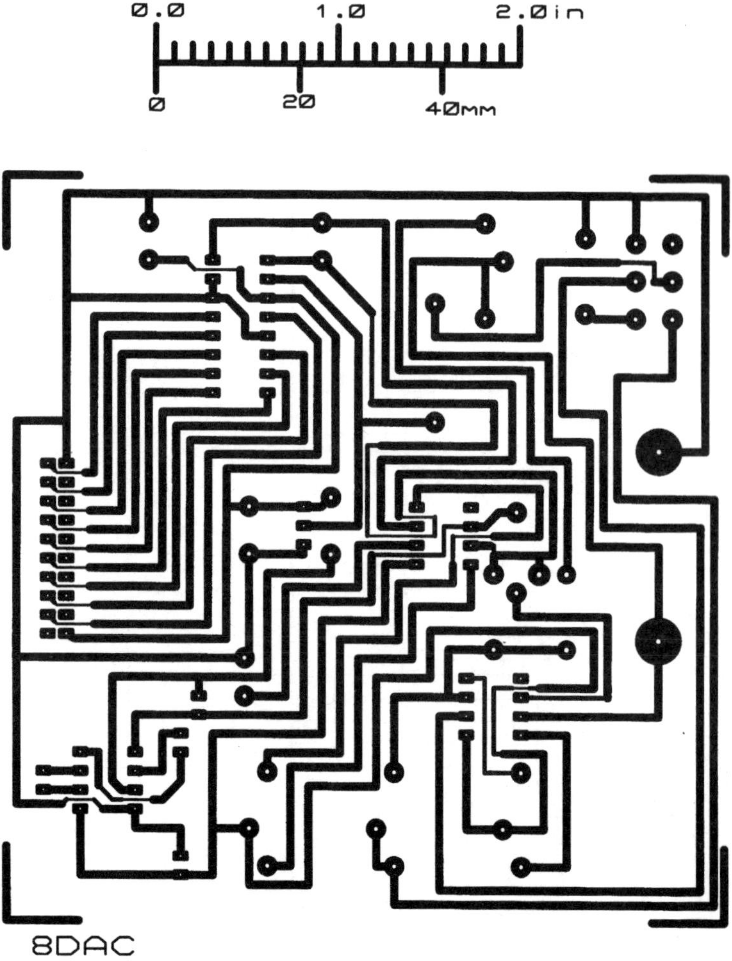

Figure A3.2 The 8DAC board PCB (Component side view)

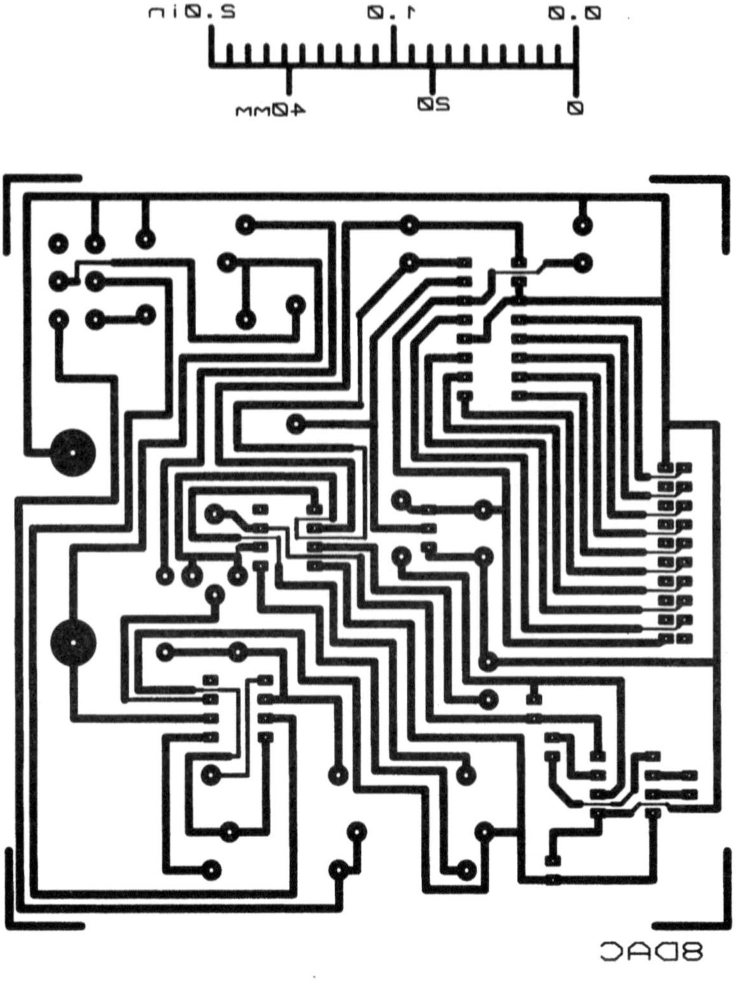

Figure A3.3 The 8DAC board PCB (Track side view)

A3.3 Components

Figure A3.4 shows the layout of the components on the board overlay.

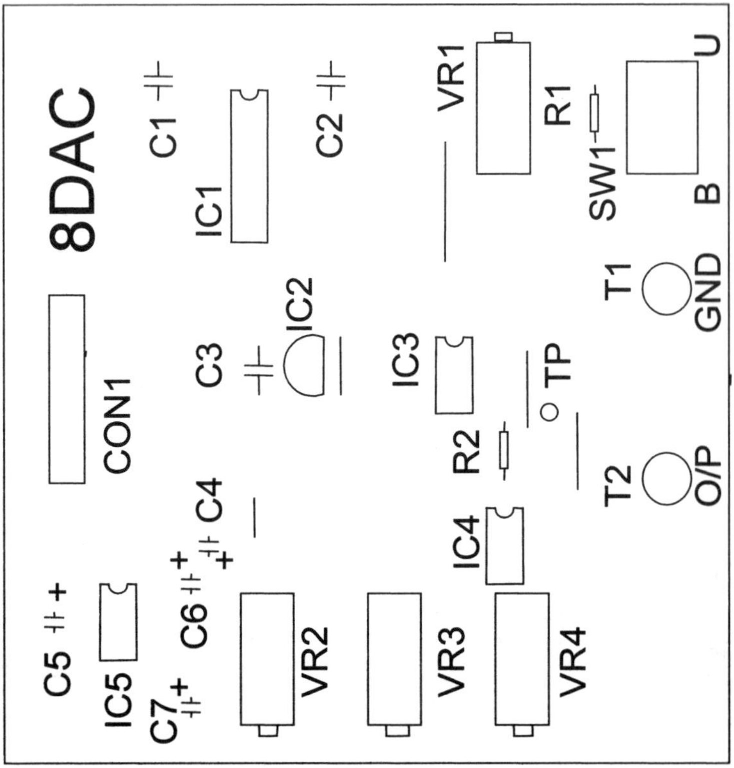

Figure A3.4 The 8DAC board component layout

Resistors

R1	4.7k	0.4W tolerance +/–5%	Farnell 332-770
R2	10k	0.4W tolerance +/–5%	Farnell 332-811

Capacitors

C1	0.1μF	multilayer ceramic	Farnell 108-925
C2	10pF	multilayer ceramic	Farnell 108-926
C3	0.1μF	multilayer ceramic	Farnell 108-925
C4	4.7μF	electrolytic (35V)	Farnell 920-575
C5	4.7μF	electrolytic (35V)	Farnell 920-575
C6	4.7μF	electrolytic (35V)	Farnell 920-575
C7	4.7μF	electrolytic (35V)	Farnell 920-575

Variable resistors

VR1	50k	18-way cermet trimmer	Farnell 306-6289
VR2	10k	18-way cermet trimmer	Farnell 306-6265
VR3	50k	18-way cermet trimmer	Farnell 306-6289
VR4	10k	18-way cermet trimmer	Farnell 306-6265

Integrated Circuits

IC1	TLC7524	8-bit DAC	Farnell 411-218
IC2	AD680	2.5V reference (TO92 package)	Farnell 411-218
IC3	TL081	Bi-FET Op Amp	Farnell 400-660
IC4	TL081	Bi-FET Op Amp	Farnell 400-660
IC5	MAX680	+5V to ±10V converter	Farnell 246-551

Switch

SW1	DPDT	rightangle	Farnell 150-209

Connectors

CON1		IDC 20-way connector	Farnell 152-279
CON2	black	4mm insulated terminal	Farnell 810-319
CON3	red	4mm insulated terminal	Farnell 810-320

A3.4 Calibration of the 8DAC board

The switch SW1 on the 8DAC board selects either the unipolar or bipolar mode. In unipolar mode an input of 0 corresponds to 0V and 255 to +5.10V. In bipolar mode the voltage range is –2.56V to +2.54 for digital inputs of 0 and 255 respectively.

An important feature of a DAC is the linearity of its output. This refers to its output voltage being directly proportional to the digital input, e.g in the unipolar mode digital inputs of 100 and 200 should give outputs of 2.00V and 4.00V respectively. In the bipolar mode 0 will give a -FSR reading (–2.56V), 128 is equivalent to 0.00V and 255 will give +FSR less the voltage equivalent of 1LSB, i.e +2.54V. The 8DAC board normally retains its calibration over a long period of time but the procedure described below should be used if recalibration is required or a different FSR is needed.

In the calibration process the 8DAC board is connected to the USB I/O 24 module in the PC using the 20 way ribbon cable. A digital voltmeter (DVM) is connected to the output terminals. Another DVM with probes will also be required. The positions of the potentiometers and other relevant connections on the 8DAC board are indicated in Figure A3.5.

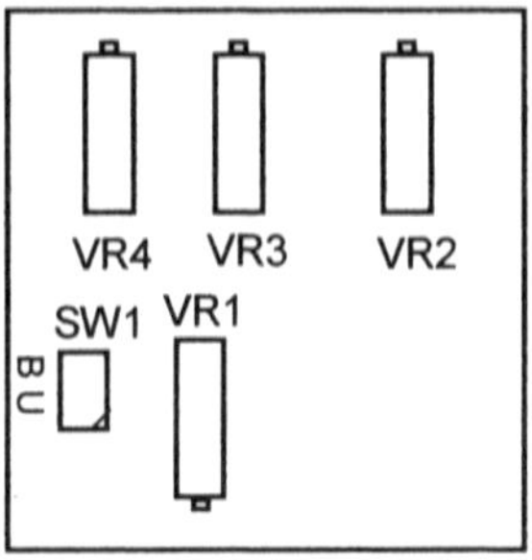

Figure A3.5 Positions of VR1-4

VR1 Unipolar -	gain	VR2 Unipolar -	zero 1
VR3 Unipolar -	zero 2	VR4 Bipolar -	+FSR

Unipolar operation

1) Connect one DVM to the output terminals of the 8DAC board.

   The respective probes of the other DVM are connected to the GND and TP (test point) terminals on the 8DAC board.

   Set switch SW1 to U and ensure that the 8DAC board is connected using the ribbon cable.

2) Run the DAC program in Chapter 6 and move the scroll bar to 0.

   Adjust VR2 until the voltage at the TP terminal is as close to 0.00V as possible.

   Adjust VR4 until the voltage output is as close to 0.00V as possible.

3) Move the scroll bar to 255 and adjust VR1 until the voltage output is 5.10V i.e. +FSR - 1 LSB.

   The linearity of the DAC board can be checked by moving the scroll bar to intermediate values between 0 and 255, i.e. 128, 64, 192, etc.

4) If necessary repeat steps 2) and 3).

Bipolar operation

This calibration should be performed after the DAC has been calibrated for unipolar operation.

1) Set the switch to B (Bipolar operation).
2) Run the program and set the scroll bar to 0.

   The output will be -FSR i.e. –2.56V.
3) Move the scroll bar to 255 and adjust VR2 to +FSR - 1LSB i.e. +2.54V.
4) The linearity of the DAC board can be checked by moving the scroll bar to intermediate values between 0 and 255, i.e. 128, 64 and 192.
5) If necessary repeat steps 3) and 4).

The voltage ranges in the bipolar mode can be altered by adjusting VR1 but this action will mean that the 8DAC board will have to be re-calibrated before using the unipolar mode again.

A3.5 Application of the 8DAC board

Once calibrated the linearity of the DAC may be checked by entering different digital inputs and noting the voltage outputs on the DVM. If a FSR less than 5.10 V is required it will be necessary to recalibrate the 8DAC board. It is unlikely that the step involving the altering of VR2 and VR3 will have to be done if FSRs are being changed.

A3.6 References

TLC5724, TLC7524E, TLC7524I 8-bit multiplying digital-to-analog converters (1998)

Texas Instruments, Post Office Box 655303, Dallas, Texas 75265, USA,

www.ti.com

AD580 Low Power, Low Cost 2.5V Reference (2001)

Analog devices, One Technology Way, PO Box 9106, Norwood, MA 01062-9106, USA

www.analog.com

MAX680 +5V to ±10V Voltage converters (1989)

Maxim Integrated Products, 120 San Gabriel Drive, Sunnyvale, CA 94086, USA

www.maxim-ic.com

TL081 Wide Bandwidth JFET Input Operational Amplifier (1995)

National Semiconductor Corporation, 1111 West Bardin Road, Arlington, Texas 76017, USA

www.National.com

A4 The 8ADC board

The 8ADC board is based upon the ADC0804 8-bit successive approximation analogue to digital converter which is manufactured by National Semiconductors, Intersil and Philips. The free running conversion time is 13690 conversions per second when the INTR (Interrupt) and WR (Write) pins are connected together. The 8ADC is used in this continuous conversion mode with the CS (Chip Select) line being used to start a new conversion by going from low to high. A conversion that is in process is halted by CS going low and the data that can be read from the output latches correspond to the data from the previously completed conversion.

The lines required for the 8ADC board are +5V, 0V, a control line to operate the CS pin and 8 data lines. These are all provided by the USB I/O 24 module connected to the USB port of the PC.

The 8ADC board may be used in either unipolar (0V to +5.10V) or bipolar (–5.12V to +5.08V) input mode. The accuracy is ±1LSB.

A4.1 The circuit

Figure A4.1 shows a schematic circuit diagram for the 8ADC board. IC1 is the ADC0804 which is an 8-bit successive approximation A to D converter with all active circuitry contained on the chip. R5 and C1 provide the self clocking for the converter and switch SW2 is used to momentarily take the INTR/WR connection to ground to ensure that the circuit starts conversion.

The analogue inputs are switchable between unipolar (0 – 5.10V) and bipolar (–5.12 – +5.08V) using SW1. The bipolar input range is accommodated by offsetting the analogue input range so that only positive input voltages are applied to the comparator.

There are no facilities to calibrate the 8ADC board and any calibration must be done in software.

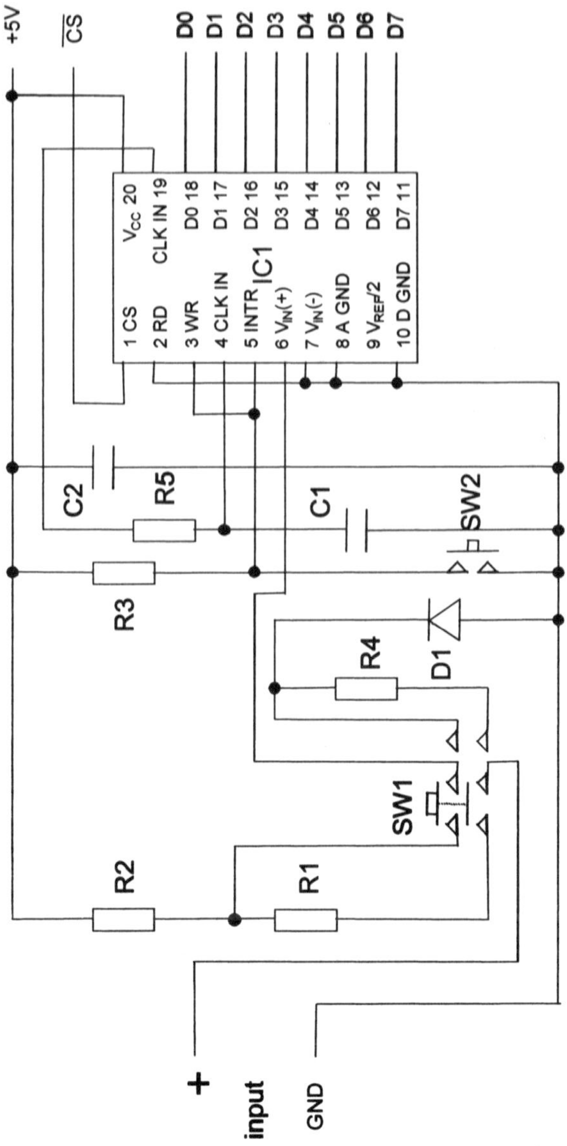

Figure A 4.1 The 8ADC board circuit

4.2 The Printed Circuit Boards

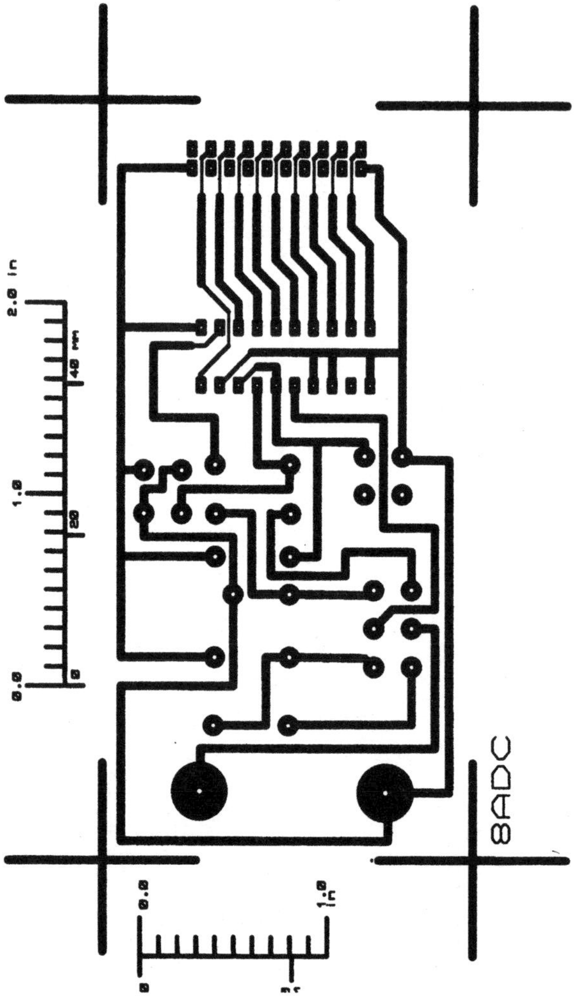

Figure A4.2 The 8ADC board PCB (Component side view)

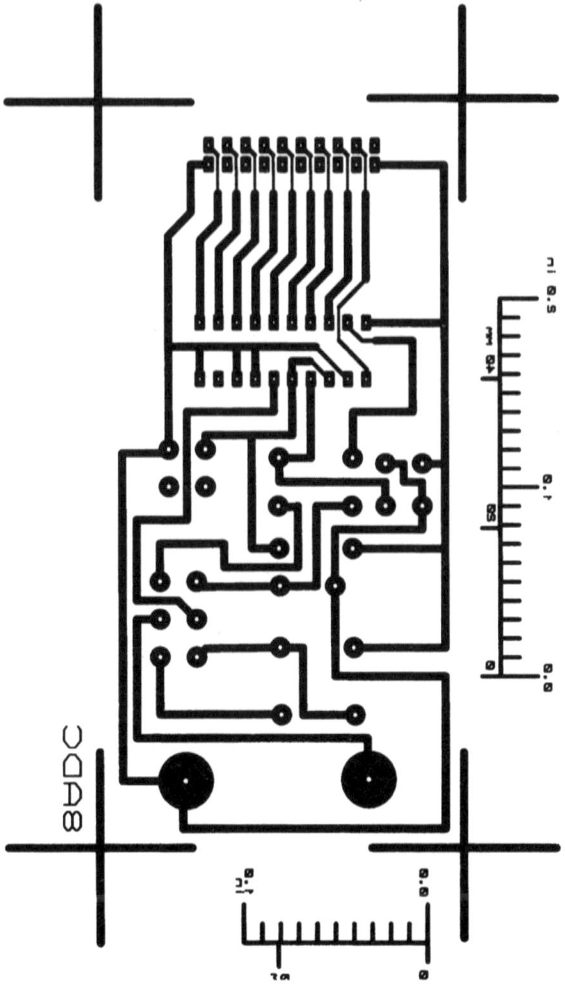

Figure A4.3 The 8ADC board PCB (Track side view)

A4.3 Components

Figure A4.4 shows the layout of the components on the board overlay.

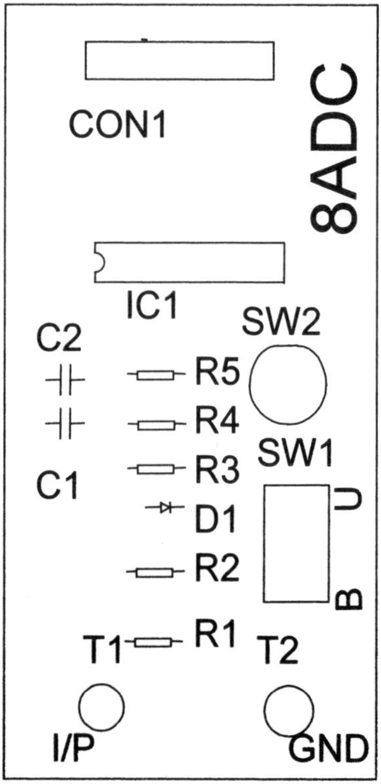

Figure A4.4 The 8ADC board component layout

Resistors

R1	10k	0.4W tolerance +/–5%	Farnell 332-811
R2	10k	0.4W tolerance +/–5%	Farnell 332-811
R3	100k	0.4W tolerance +/–5%	Farnell 332-938
R4	220R	0.4W tolerance +/–5%	Farnell 332-616
R5	10k	0.4W tolerance +/–5%	Farnell 332-811

Capacitors

C1	150pF	Dipped radial multi-layered ceramic	Farnell 647-755
C2	0.1μF	multilayer ceramic	Farnell 108-925

Diodes

D1	1N4148	signal diode	Farnell 885-660

Integrated Circuit

IC1	ADC0804	8-bit ADC	Farnell 396-187

Switches

SW1	DPDT	switch	Farnell 150-209
SW2	SPNO	momentary switch	Farnell 151-137

Connectors

CON1		IDC 20-way connector	Farnell 152-279
T1	black	4mm insulated terminal	Farnell 810-319
T2	red	4mm insulated terminal	Farnell 810-320

A4.4 Calibration of the 8ADC board

The calibration of the 8ADC has to be performed using the 8adc.vbp program. It is necessary to alter the corresponding full scale (FS) values in both the unipolar and bipolar modes. This is done in the Display routine.

```
Private Sub Display()
'Select equivalent voltage settings
If Polarity = 0 Then
invalvolt = (5.10 * inval) / 255
Else
invalvolt = (inval - 128) * 5.12/ 128
End If
'Display ADC decimal reading
Text1.Text = Str$(inval)
'Display ADC voltage reading
Text2.Text = Format$(invalvolt, "##.##")
End Sub
```

The shaded portions of the code show where the changes must be made. The first one refers to the unipolar FS, the second one to the bipolar FS.

The FS values are determined by finding the input voltages which just cause the decimal output of the 8ADC board to change from 254 to 255. The accuracy with which the value can be determined is affected by the sensitivity of the measuring voltmeter and how smoothly the output of the power supply can be changed. The procedure will have be carried out separately for both the unipolar and bipolar modes, and the measured values will replace the 5.10 and 5.12 values shown in the shaded portions of the code.

This type of calibration cannot accommodate any zero offset or non-linearity that may be present but it can be an improvement upon the values that are already in use in the program.

A4.5 Reference

ADC080803/0804 CMOS 8-bit A/D converters Data sheet (17 Oct 2002)

Philips Semiconductors, Koninklijke Philips Electronics NV , www.semiconductors.philips.com

A5 The 12ADC board

The 12ADC board is a 12 bit analogue to digital converter which can be used in the range of ±4.095V. It may be used with the USB I/O 24 module attached to the USB port of the PC. The board is based upon an ICL7109CPL device which has an auto zero facility and outputs its digital data in a high and low byte format. The high byte contains bits signifying polarity, overrange and the 4 most significant bits of digital data and the low byte has the 8 remaining bits of data. Chapter 8 provides extensive details of how the 12-bit digital data is taken from this ADC.

A5.1 The circuit

The ICL7109CPL dual-ramp integrating A to D converter outputs its digital signal in two bytes i.e. Hi and Lo. The circuit shown in Figure A5.1 has to enable the data to be extracted such that it is not corrupted when only 8 data lines and 2 control lines are used. This is put into practice using IC3 (a dual D type flip flop). All of the circuitry to the right of IC1 provides the necessary clocking and integrating circuits and the reference sources. It also provides the analogue inputs. IC4 provides the necessary –5V for IC1.

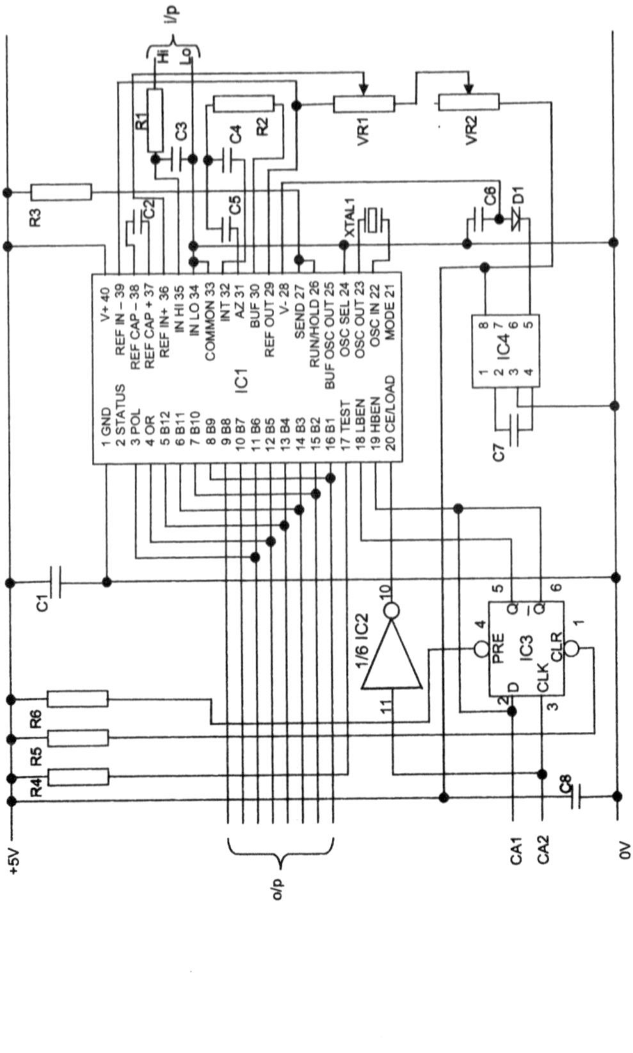

Figure A5.1 The 12ADC board circuit

A5.2 The Printed Circuit Boards

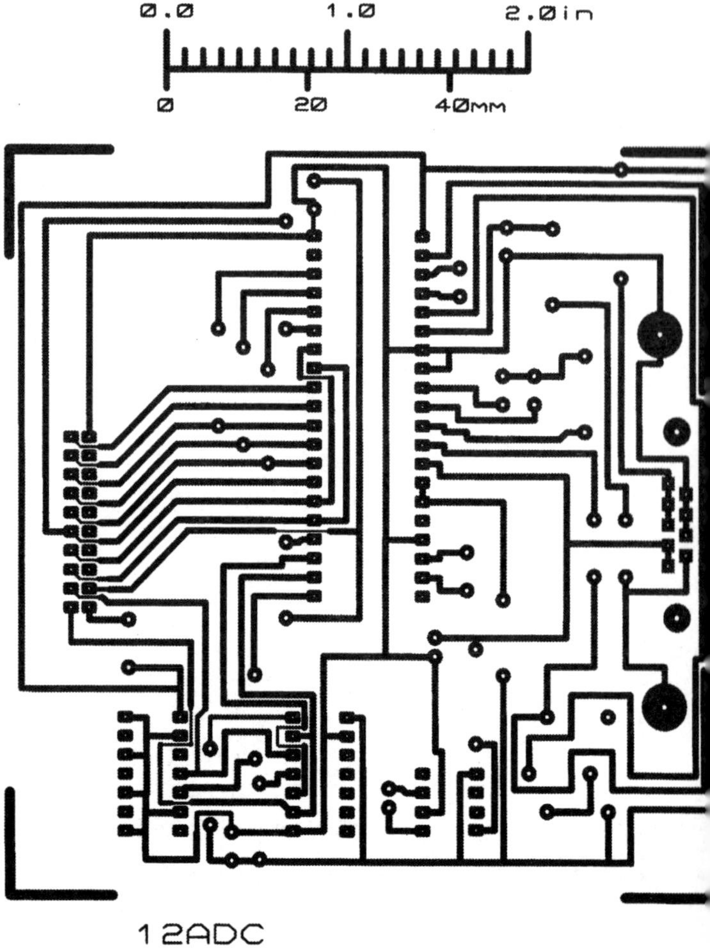

Figure A5.2 The 12ADC board PCB (Component side view)

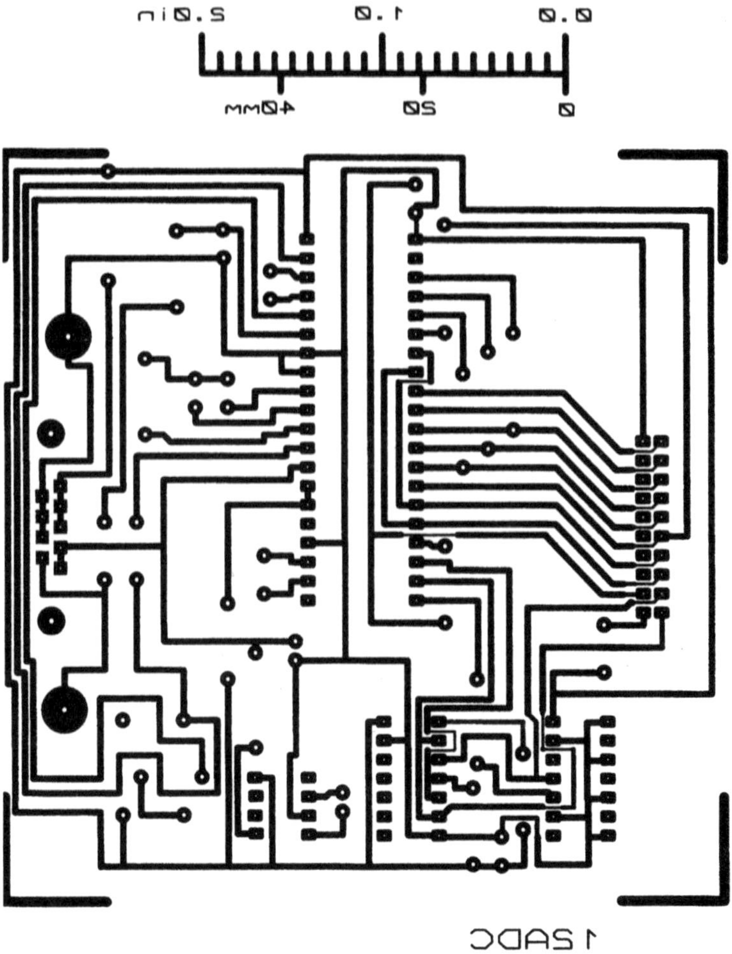

Figure A5.3 The 12ADC board PCB (Track side view)

A5.3 Components

Figure A5.4 shows the layout of the components on the board overlay.

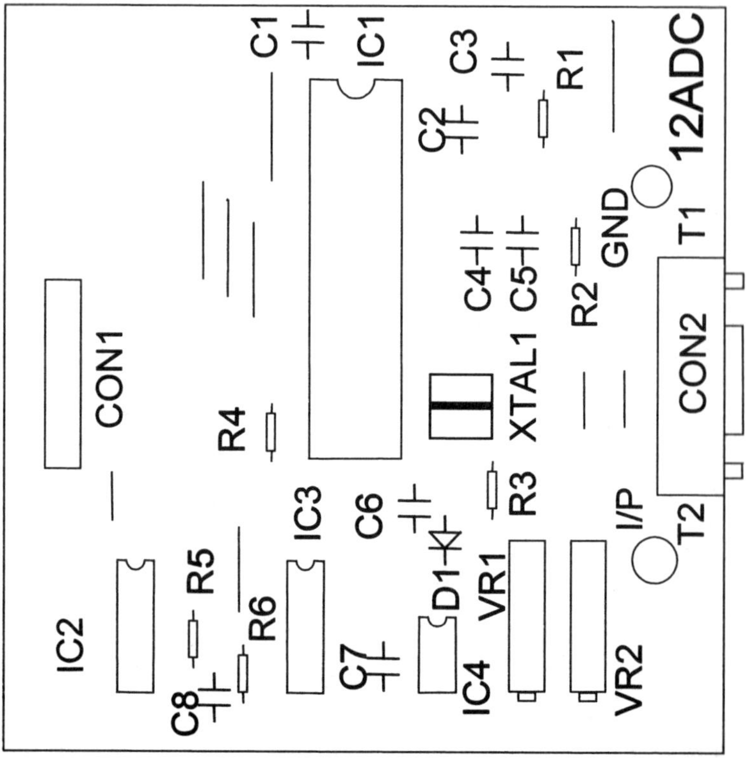

Figure A5.4 The 12ADC board component layout

Resistors

R1	1M	0.4W tolerance +/–5%	Farnell 333-050
R2	200k	0.4W tolerance +/–5%	Farnell 332-811
R3	1k	0.4W tolerance +/–5%	Farnell 332-690
R4	1k	0.4W tolerance +/–5%	Farnell 332-690
R5	1k	0.4W tolerance +/–5%	Farnell 332-690
R6	1k	0.4W tolerance +/–5%	Farnell 332-690

Capacitors

C1	0.1μF	multilayer ceramic	Farnell 108-925
C2	1μF	miniature layer	RS 114-430
C3	0.01μF	monolithic ceramic	Farnell 430-559
C4	0.15μF	polyester	Farnell 143-681
C5	0.33μF	polyester	Farnell 143-683
C6	10μF	electrolytic (50V)	Farnell 383-7117
C7	10μF	electrolytic (50V)	Farnell 383-7117
C8	0.1μF	multilayer ceramic	Farnell 108-926

Variable resistors

VR1	1k	18-way cermet trimmer	Farnell 306-6230
VR2	50k	18-way cermet trimmer	Farnell 306-6289

Diode

D1	OA47	signal diode	Farnell 306-003

Integrated Circuits

IC1	ICL7109	12-bit ADC	Farnell 335-7601
IC2	74LS04	Hex inverters	Farnell 373-400
IC3	74LS74	D trigger flip flops	Farnell 374-027
IC4	ICL7660	voltage converter	Farnell 408-566

Crystal

XTAL1	3.579MHz	crystal HC18/U	Farnell 170-229

Connectors

CON1		IDC 20-way connector	Farnell 152-279
CON2		9-way D-type socket	Farnell 737-579
T1	black	4mm insulated terminal	Farnell 810-319
T2	red	4mm insulated terminal	Farnell 810-320

A5.4 Calibration of the 12ADC board

The auto zero facility of the ICL7109CPL means that there is no zero adjustment on the board. The only adjustment necessary is the Gain range and this is achieved using two variable resistors VR1 and VR2 (Figure A5.5).

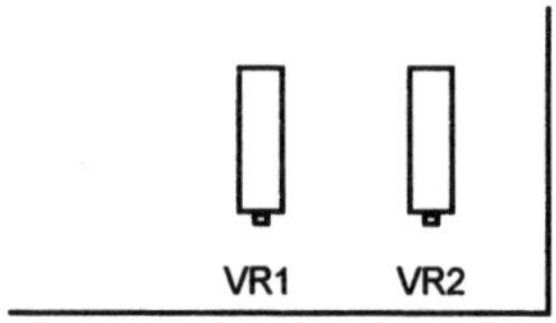

Figure A5.5 Positions of VR1 and VR2

Each of these variable resistors requires 18 turns to alter the resistance from its maximum to minimum value. VR2 should be initially set to its mid-value, i.e. 9 turns from either extremity. The calibration procedure then requires the use of a variable voltage laboratory power supply (0 to

10V) and a DVM which has a resolution of 1mV. If +2.000V is applied to the 12ADC board, VR1 and VR2 can be adjusted such that 2000 appears on the 12ADC Form when the program 12adc.vbp is used. It is useful to check the linearity of the board by varying the input voltage and noting the digital output. This should also be done for a negative voltage input.

A5.5 Reference

ICL7109 12 Bit Binary A/D Converter with 3-state Binary Outputs

Maxim Integrated Products, 120 San Gabriel Drive, Sunnyvale, CA 94086, USA

www.maxim-ic.com

A6 The VGPA board

This board is designed to be used in conjunction with the 12ADC board and increases the sensitivity of the 12-bit ADC of that board. The board contains a preamplifier input stage which has a gain that can be set to x1, x10, x100 and x1000. This gives the following voltage ranges:

x1	–4.095V	to	+4.095V
x10	–409.5mV	to	+409.5mV
x100	–40.95mV	to	+40.95mV
x1000	–4.095mV	to	+4.095mV

Table A6.1

The programs used with the combined boards are identical to those used with the 12ADC, with slight modifications in the FSR to account for the voltage range that is being used.

A6.1 Making connections to the VGPA board

There are 3 inputs to the VGPA board, a positive signal input, a negative signal input and a ground line (Figure A6.1).

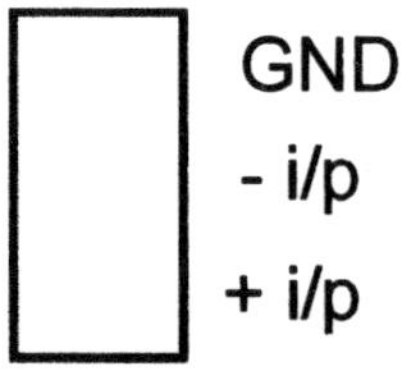

Figure A6.1 Inputs to the VGPA board

In most circumstances it is necessary to connect the GND and -I/P together. The signal input should then be connected to between the -I/P and +I/P lines. The board is connected to the 12ADC board using the 15-pin D type connector.

Selecting the gain

The gain of the VGPA board is achieved by jumpers A, B and C on the board. These are situated close to the input terminals and require the jumper connections to be made according to Figure A6.2.

o o A

o o B

o o C

Gain	Connection
x1	None
x10	A
x100	B
x1000	C

Figure A6.2 Selecting the gain

A6.2 The circuit

The VGPA board is based upon the AD524 precision instrumentation amplifier. Figure A6.3 shows a schematic of the board. The ±15V supply is provided by the voltage converter IC2. VR1 and VR2 are used to provide input and output offset. The gain of the board is altered using jumpers on CON4. The analogue input can be allowed to float by removing the jumper at CON2.

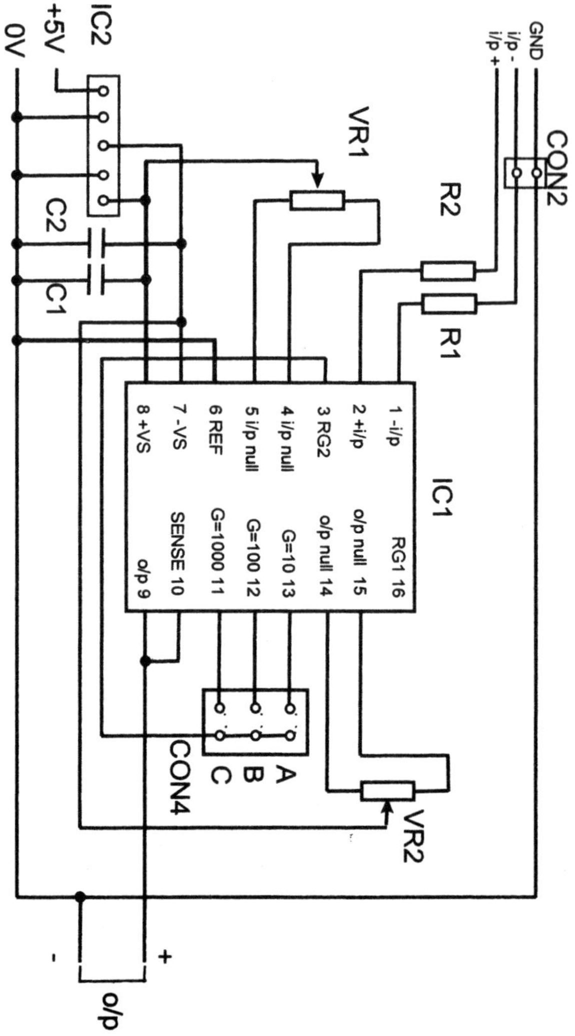

Figure A6.3 The VGPA board circuit

A6.3 The Printed Circuit Boards

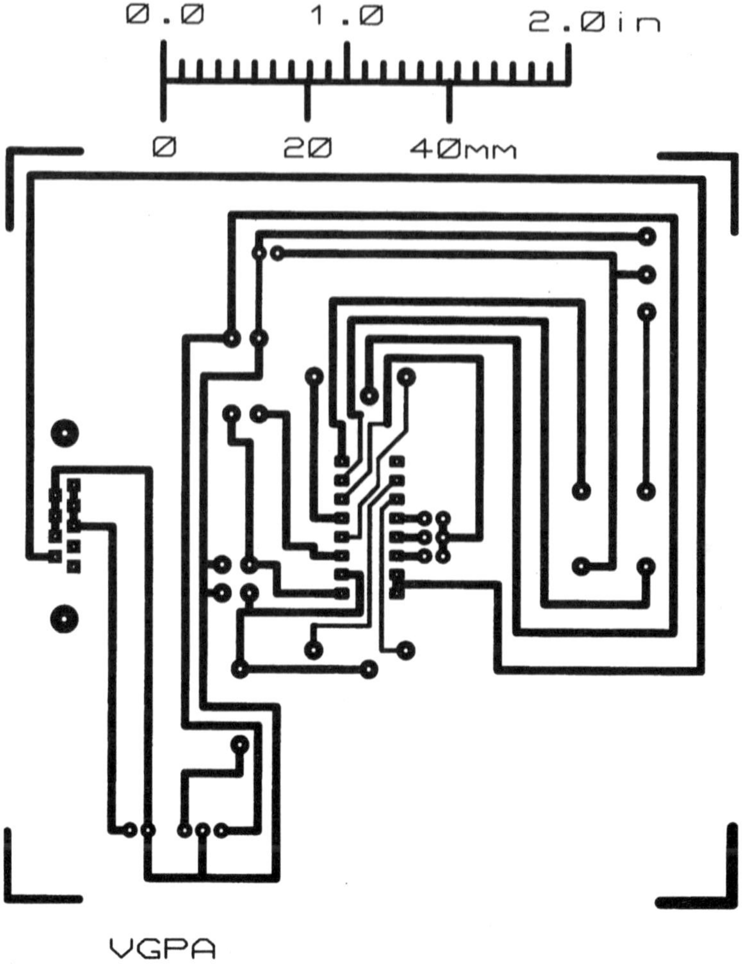

Figure A6.4 The VGPA PCB (Component side view)

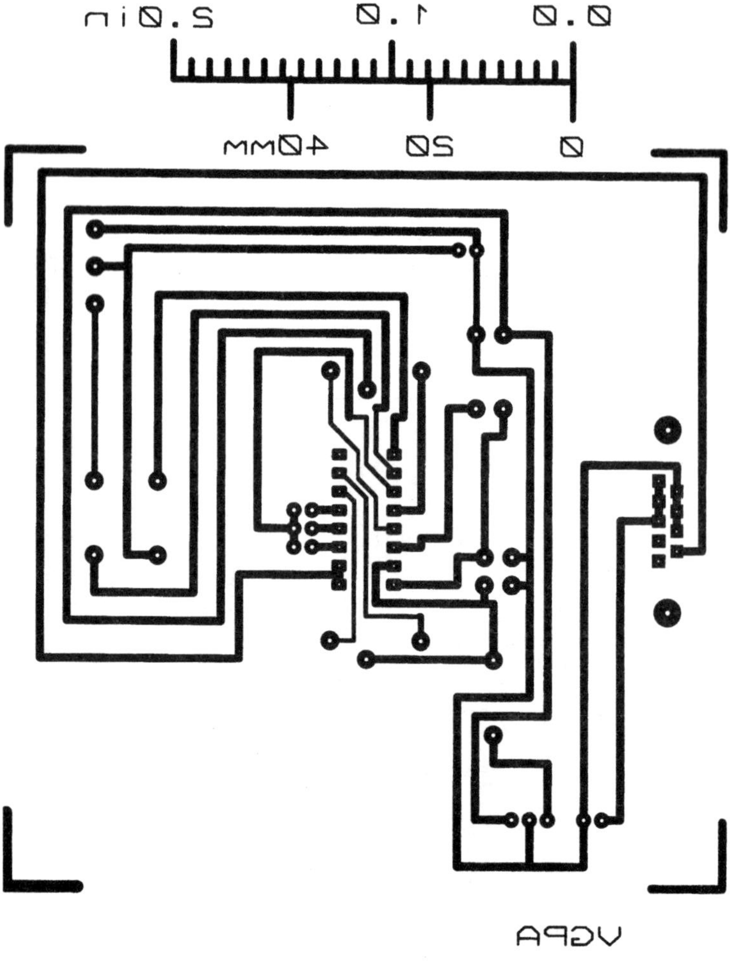

Figure A6.5 The VGPA PCB (Track side view)

A6.4 Components

Figure A6.6 shows the layout of the components on the board overlay.

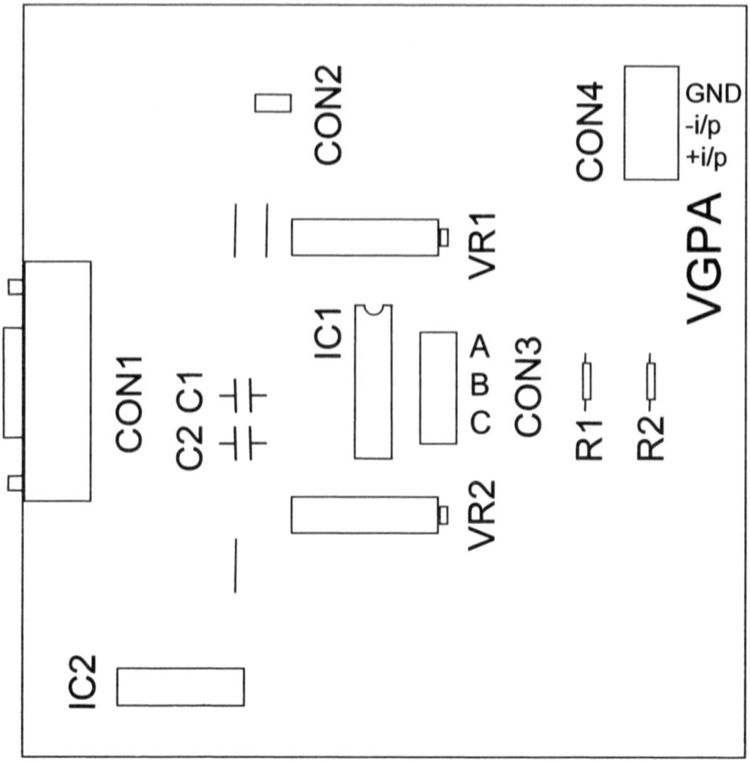

Figure A6.6 The VGPA board component layout

Resistors

R1	10k	0.4W tolerance +/–5%	Farnell 332-811
R2	10k	0.4W tolerance +/–5%	Farnell 332-811

Capacitors

C1	0.01μF	multilayer ceramic	Farnell 430-559
C2	0.01μF	multilayer ceramic	Farnell 430-559

Variable resistors

VR1	10k	18-way cermet trimmer	Farnell 306-6265
VR2	10k	18-way cermet trimmer	Farnell 306-6265

Integrated Circuits

IC1	AD524AD	Instrumentation amp	Farnell 402-138
IC2	NMA0515D	dc to dc converter	Farnell 330-760
	(Newport)	5 to +/ –15V	

Connectors

CON1		9-way D-type plug	Farnell 637-531
CON2		1+1 pcb pin-strip header	Farnell 143-132
CON3		3-way pcb mted screw terminal	Farnell 101-785
CON4		3+3 pcb pin-strip header	Farnell 621-857
	2 off	jumper link	Farnell 150-410

A6.5 Calibration of the VGPA

The VGPA is calibrated in two stages. Initially the gain of the ICL7109CPL analogue to digital converter is adjusted on the 12ADC board and then the input and output offsets of the AD524 on the VGPA board are adjusted.

Stage 1

The 12ADC board should be initially calibrated using the instructions in Section A5.

Stage 2

The laboratory power supply should now be connected to the +I/P and -I/P terminals of the VGPA board. If the AD524 is connected for high gain it may be necessary to use a potential divider across the output terminals of the laboratory power supply (Figure A6.7).

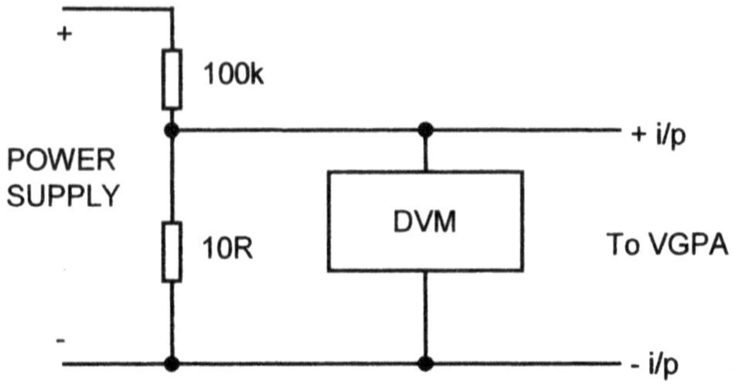

Figure A6.7 Method of obtaining very small voltages

The only controls that must be altered now are VR1 and VR2 on the VGPA board (Figure A6.8). A known voltage is applied to the VGPA. If the gain of the AD524 is high, VR1 (input offset) is adjusted first followed by VR2 (output offset) until the input voltage and digital output agree. If the gain is low VR2 is adjusted first followed by VR1.

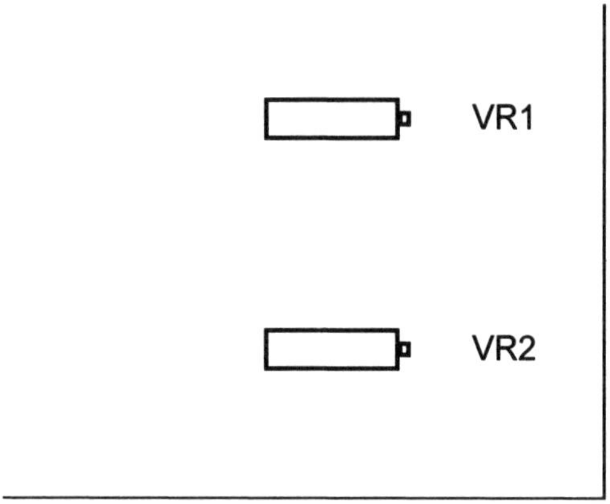

Figure A6.8 Positions of VR1 and VR2

A6.6 References

AD524 Precision Instrumentation Amplifier

Analog Devices, One Technology Way, PO Box 9106, Norwood, MA 01062-9106, USA

www.analog.com

A7 Suppliers

The components used in the circuit boards described above may be obtained from the following suppliers in the UK:

RS

RS Components Ltd, PO Box 99, Corby, Northants, NN17 9RS

Tel: 01536 201201; Fax: 01536 201501

http://rswww.com

Farnell

Farnell Electronic Components Ltd, Canal Road, Leeds, LS12 2TU

Tel: 0113 263 6311; Fax: 0113 263 3411

www.farnell.com/uk

The supplier of the USB I/O 24 module is:

Alpha Micro Components Ltd, Springfield House, Cranes Road, Sherbourne St John, Basingstoke, Hants, RG24 9LJ

Tel: 01256 851770; Fax: 01256 851771

www.alphamicro.net

Bibliography

Books

Francesco Balena, *Programming Microsoft Visual Basic 6.0*, (1999), Microsoft

Evangelos Petroutsos and Kevin Hough, *Visual Basic 6 Developer's Handbook,* (1999), Sybex

Eric A Smith, Valor Whisler and Hank Marquis, *Visual Basic 6 Bible,* (1998), IDG Books

G B Clayton, *Data Converters*, (1982), Macmillan Education

Devices

Many of the data sheets can be downloaded from the relevant manufacturers or suppliers web sites:

Analog Devices

www.analog.com

Elexol Pty Ltd

www.elexol.com

Farnell Electronic Components

www.farnell.com/uk

Future Devices Technology International Ltd

www.ftdichip.com

Bibliography

Maxim Integrated Products

www.maxim-ic.com

National Semiconductor Corporation

www.National.com

Philips Semiconductors

www.semiconductors.philips.com

RS Components Ltd

http://rswww.com

Ravar Pty Ltd

www.ravar.net

Texas Instruments

www.ti.com

Index

Note